AN INNOCENT AT POLEBROOK

A MEMOIR OF AN 8TH AIR FORCE BOMBARDIER

BY

CHARLES N. STEVENS

To Harry
Best Wishes
Charles N. Stevens
351st Bomb Group

This book is a work of non-fiction. Names and places have been changed to protect the privacy of all individuals. The events and situations are true.

© 2003, 2004 by Charles N. Stevens.
All rights reserved.

ISBN: 1-4140-4564-6 (e-book)
ISBN: 1-4140-4563-8 (Paperback)

Library of Congress Control Number: 2003099051

This book is printed on acid free paper.

Printed in the United States of America
Bloomington, IN

1stBooks - rev. 01/19/04

TABLE OF CONTENTS

INTRODUCTION

The following is an account of my experiences as a bombardier in the U. S. 8th Air Force, 351st Bomb Group, 509th Squadron, flying with Lieutenant Johnston's crew in England during the summer and early fall of 1944. Airmen from different crews or bomber groups would naturally have their own versions of events because of their unique experiences and their individual reactions to them. Even the men on our own bomber might vary in their perceptions. Their core experiences, however, would be quite similar. This is my story, from my point of view.

What I have written is not intended to be a history of the 8th Air Force or the 351st Bomb Group. I leave that to the historians. The progress of the war can be gleaned only from scattered statements throughout as they relate directly to our missions.

Very little has been left out. Failures and inadequacies find their way into the material as well as successes and strengths. Everyone's life, in or out of war, is a mixture of these, and we were simply ordinary people caught up in extraordinary events.

Some men endured much more terrifying experiences than I, many of them from our field, and some faced less. Those who were shot down, ended up in German prison camps or were rescued by the underground had far more chilling tales to tell. This is simply my narrative about my experiences, written without any desire to compare them with anyone else's.

* * *

Had I known 57years ago that I would someday write about our missions, I would have kept a diary or a detailed journal, but all I had with me when I left England was a typed list of my missions provided by the field and a mind seething with a collage of visions. Over the years some of those pictures have mellowed softly into vague memories. Some I can still vividly recall, but others have dimmed or have faded away altogether.

After the war, I wanted to forget about combat, put it out of my mind so that I could go about living a normal life. Except for a few haunting recollections that stole into my consciousness during idle moments, I was able to keep the rest at bay.

Now, at 78 in 2003 I realize that I had simply walked away from it all, hadn't really dealt with the war. Also, with the proper perspective of passing time, I realized that I was once a very tiny part of history. I thought that those who came after me, my great grandchildren and great great grandchildren, might want to know about my experiences, just as I would have wanted to know about those of family members who had come before me.

With only my list of missions and my memories, I was in no position to write about my experiences. I also had a collection of letters that I had written to my parents from "Somewhere in England," but they contained nothing about the missions since we were not allowed to write anything about them. The letters did provide, however, information about life on the base, my health and morale, movies we had seen, thoughts about home, our passes and leaves.

Although I could connect some of my vivid memories with particular missions, others floated off, unattached to any specific one. They were over five decades old and subject to all the distortions that time can inflict.

I knew that if I were to write about the experiences, I would have to have more information about them, real written facts and documents to bring discipline and order to my memories. The National Archives in Washington, D. C. provided what I needed. On two different occasions I spent a total of five full days in the National Archives at Suitland, Maryland and the new facility at College Park, Maryland poring over the records of the 351st Bomb Group. I opened neat folders for each of my missions, the records comprised of mission reports, route maps, damage reports, bombardier's narratives, weather information and many other papers. I filled up notebook paper with notes on each raid and photocopied all mission reports and route maps as well as any other papers that were pertinent. Armed with these documents, personal letters and my memories, many refreshed by the documents, I began writing, recreating the missions and my life at Polebrook.

After losing track of my crew, I discovered only a few years ago that our pilot, Harry Johnston, lived in Phoenix, Arizona. It was with great pleasure that I contacted him and arranged to meet him in Phoenix. We had a wonderful conversation of several hours in which we renewed our friendship and talked about not only our lives, but also our missions so many years ago. It surprised me how many of our memories were exactly the same. He was of great help in restoring fragments of experiences I had lost, or in restructuring them from his perspective as a pilot. His input was very helpful in rounding out some of the accounts.

The material has been written from the point of view of the 19-year-old I was at that time—at least as much as possible, considering the vast amount of time between now and when I flew. In constructing a true picture of that time period, I have had to swallow my pride several times, writing about embarrassing moments as well as ones about which I am proud.

I have written in first person, present tense so that, even though the events occurred many years ago, the reader might feel that he is in the present, that he has turned the calendar back 57 years, and rides with me in the nose of the B-17.

In some instances where the use of actual names might be sensitive, I have changed them or left them out. Any dialogue is constructed from memory and contains the actual thrust of what was said, even if the words are not exact. Other dialogue is supplied to make the story clearer or to convey information.

It is important to bear in mind also that rumors and hearsay were as much a part of my reality as fact during that time. My perceptions were always a blend of these.

I have changed a great deal over the years, the influences of education, knowledge, time and experience gradually shaping me into a different person from that innocent young man who flew during the war, who knew so very little about life. In other ways, I am exactly the same. I still don't hate anybody or any group. I try to get along with people, and I love my family, my state and my country.

I would like to thank my wonderful wife, Dolores Seidman, for reading all of this material several times—checking for typing errors, misspellings, grammatical mistakes, wordiness, unclear sentences, word order and general understanding. She never reads accounts about war and detests violence of any kind, so her reading through all this was an act of love that I greatly appreciate.

I would also like to thank the members of my writing group who critiqued each story, caught errors in punctuation, word order, word repetition and redundancies—who wouldn't even allow a comma out of place. I would especially like to thank Bill Robbins, Carole Kretzer, Betty Lou Miley, Louise Tang, Marie Summers, Rosemary Reuter, Betty Sheridan, Jeanne Smillie, Rosalie Matlovsky, and John Landrum. A special thanks to all of them for their encouragement.

SOME BACKGROUND INFORMATION

The early bombing missions during 1942 and 1943, before I arrived in England, had been near-disasters. The losses were so high that, at times, the generals wondered whether daylight precision bombing was feasible. The average number of missions flown by a crew before they were shot down was 11. Unless the crew was lucky, like that of the *Memphis Belle* who completed all of their 25 missions, they would eventually be shot down.

The odds were heavily in favor of the enemy. The Americans flew into hostile territory virtually unprotected and with very few bombers, allowing the German flak gunners and the Luftwaffe to concentrate on them. The bomber crews battled hordes of fighters with inadequate armament.

As bomber production grew in the United States and the Air Force trained an increasing number of crews, the 8th Air Force was not only able to cope with their losses, but also to increase the number of planes available for missions. New air bases were opened and new groups were formed. With more bombers carrying improved fire power, the odds began to change. American fighter planes could escort them long distances, and the Luftwaffe began to suffer significant losses.

By the time I arrived in England in the summer of 1944 the 8th Air Force could mount missions of 1100 planes protected by fighter escorts to and from the target, even over it. The odds had turned greatly in our favor with many more crews finishing their required 25 missions. Conditions were so improved that a tour of duty was raised to 30 missions. Near the end of my tour it was raised to 35. German flak gunners had so many planes to contend with that they could not shoot effectively at all of them. The Luftwaffe generally struck when there were lapses in fighter cover or when the bomber formations became disorganized or scattered. They also finished off any plane so damaged by flak that it had to drop out of formation. Instead of attacking individually as they had earlier, the Messerschmitt 109s and Focke-Wulf 190s struck suddenly in tight formations with concentrated firepower.

Even though the odds were better when I arrived, flak over the targets was still murderous, and the Luftwaffe was still capable of sneaking in between our fighter protection and wreaking havoc very quickly. Many planes were still being shot down. During my tour of duty, from June 14 to September 22, 1944, the 8th Air Force lost 810 heavy bombers, 495 B-17s and 315 B-24s. During the same period we lost 31 planes from our field at Polebrook. On a single day, September 12, 1944, the 8th Air Force lost 35 planes, most of them B-17s, on the raid to Ruhland, Germany, 6 of those belonging to our group. *

*Based on statistics from *The Mighty Eighth War Diary* by Roger Freeman.

FORMATIONS

The area north of London, particularly the part of eastern England that bulges toward the English Channel, was dotted with airfields during World War II. Most of these were used by the 8th Air Force. The airfield for the 351st Bomb Group at Polebrook, located southwest of Peterborough, was only one of many.

The 8th Air Force bomb groups were divided into three <u>divisions</u>. The 1st and 3rd Divisions were comprised of B-17s, the 2nd Division of B-24s. Our bomb group, the 351st, was a part of the 1st Division.

The divisions were divided into smaller units called <u>combat wings</u>. Within our division there were four of these. The 351st Bomb Group belonged to the 94th. Generally a Combat Wing was comprised of three <u>groups</u>, each from a different field.

The 351st Bomb Group at Polebrook was further divided into four <u>squadrons</u>, the men in each occupying different barracks. The four squadrons were the 508th, 509th to which our crew belonged, 510th and 511th.

During a typical mission three of our squadrons would fly, the other one "standing down." Generally 12 planes would fly from each squadron so that our combat group was comprised of 36 planes. All 36 planes would take off one after the other and fly to a designated rendezvous point in England, at an assigned altitude where they would gradually gather into the combat formation.

Each of the three squadrons would be assigned a certain altitude. The lead squadron or lead <u>box</u> might fly over the target at 26,100 feet. The high box would fly 600 feet above them and slightly behind at 26,700 feet and the low box 600 feet below and slightly behind at 25,500 feet. The boxes were also staggered laterally so that none would be directly below another.

Once our group had assembled we would join the other two in our wing, making a total of 108 planes. Our wing would then take its place in a parade of others, the number determined by the type of target and the tonnage of bombs to be dropped.

SLEET

Sleet like grains of rice bounces and rolls crazily on the wooden steps of the Officers Club. I'd never seen the stuff before and had certainly never expected it in May, but winters last a long time in Newfoundland. Podoske, the co-pilot on our crew, and I tramp up the few steps in our heavy shoes, scattering some of the granules, popping others beneath our soles. Angry gray clouds tumble over the air base, borne on the same chill wind that numbs our faces, and drives the bits of ice against the building.

The warm, noisy, alcoholic breath of the club meets us at the door as the arctic air attempts to sweep in with us, only to be shut off by the slamming door. A group of officers are gathered around the bar, the smoke from their cigarettes rising in lazy curls as they sip their bourbon. Some, with their elbows on the bar, turn their heads at odd angles to listen to those standing near them. A few who'd been drinking the longest slur their words, the moist fingers of alcohol having turned their volumes up a notch and stroked their lips with anesthesia.

Several men at the Ping-Pong tables paddle the celluloid ball back and forth, filling the room with their hollow metronome-like sounds, the regular ka-plink-ka-plunk, ka-plink-ka-plunk of their playing.

"Come on. Stevens. Let's have a drink," says Podoske.

"No. You know I don't drink. I really don't want any."

"Come on.   Just this once before we go overseas."

"I just don't want a drink, Podoske", I say, feeling uncomfortable about being asked.

He turns toward the bar, muttering, "Well, damn it, I'm going to have one."

Rubenstein, one of the other bombardiers, walks from the bar toward me with a small glass of whisky in his hand.

"Hey, Stevens, how about a game of Ping-Pong?"

His lips are already lazy. I don't know how many he's downed.

"Yeah, sure," I reply as I grab the paddles and ball.

Rubenstein sets his full glass on top of a low shelf and readies himself to play. At first we slide into the regular rhythm of the game, ka-plink-ka-plunk, ka-plink-ka-plunk. Each time one of us scores a point, and just before we begin the serve, he reaches for his drink.   At first the game's even, but as the play progresses, and he continues nipping, his shots become less accurate. I begin to score more as he struggles to hit the ball and eventually keep his balance. I'm like a fighter taking advantage of a wounded man. He finally swings wildly at the ball, staggers backward then leans forward, holding on to the table for stability. Hopelessly beaten and barely able to stand, he skids his paddle on the table and slurs, "Aw the hell with it!" and walks unsteadily back to the bar.

Uncomfortable at the Officers Club, I decide to return to the barracks. Podoske waves to me from the bar as I leave. I thrust my hands in my pockets and hunch my shoulders against the cold wind as I walk back. The sleet has stopped, but the persistent clouds block out the stars. Even though I wince at the icy breeze, I'm glad to be out of the acrid cigarette smoke and the sweet smell of bourbon that had saturated the Officers Club. I liked the men, but I'd always been uneasy around drunkenness and the kind of uninhibited, unpredictable wildness it releases. The lights on the air base twinkle in the clear, fresh air, and the lighted squares of windows stand out sharply.

Trudging up the shadowed stairway to the second story of the barracks, I open the door, walk into our dark room. The officers on our crew had been assigned to a cubicle-like space just large enough for two double-deck bunk beds, a chair and a small table. The beds are all neatly made with stretched olive drab blankets on top. Johnston, our pilot, and Warren, our navigator, are off on the base somewhere.

I sit down at the table in the dimly lighted room, wishing that I could write a letter home, but now that we are headed overseas, I can't tell my family where I am or what I've been doing. The dull quarters close down on me. I'm lonely. The silence reminds me how different I am from the others who now revel in the Officers Club. I get along well with all of them except at times like these. I yearn to write to my parents, to touch in some way those I love and who love me the way I am.

* * *

Much had happened before we arrived here at Gander. I wrote them about leaving Alexandria, Louisiana late in the afternoon on a troop train with the send-off band playing "I'll be Glad When You're Dead You Rascal You" as a kind of morbid joke. I also wrote them about Podoske and his sandwiches. He brought some along, warning us that we'd better buy our own because we wouldn't be fed on the train. We teased him about being so worried, but he insisted he was right and further warned us that we shouldn't ask him for any of his. He had looked out after himself, and we should have taken care of ourselves.

I hadn't told them what happened later. Podoske was right. As we sped north out of Louisiana, and the skies darkened, we had begun to feel hungry. There was no word about any dinner. He unwrapped one of his sandwiches, and smugly bit into it. Warren said, "Surely you're not going to eat that in front of us, and not give us any".

"I warned you guys", spluttered Podoske, "I told you guys to get your own before we ever started out!"

He ate his sandwich with a kind of superior but indignant look on his face.

"We're hungry Podoske, and as a member of the crew, I think you should share them with us", Johnston said.

"I warned you", he blurted between bites.

I also added my plea, asking him for just one bite. We watched him eat, but he became very uncomfortable. We continued to beg softly as he gradually began to squirm.

4

"Oh for Christ sake! Damn it! Take half of this one. Divide it among yourselves. Next time maybe you'll be better prepared!"

We accepted the remnant and split it up among us, laughing at Podoske who saw nothing funny about it.

The troop train had taken us to Kearny, Nebraska where we were, in a few days, to ferry a B-17 bomber to England. Nebraska was hot and dry with thunderstorms in the afternoons that hurled lightning bolts all around the field. Some of the crews took off early for the East Coast, but our plane, suffering from a malfunction of the de-icing boots on the leading edges of its wings, sat in a hanger several days while mechanics hovered over the problem.

With the de-icing mechanism repaired we flew eastward in the brand new plane to the airbase at Manchester, New Hampshire where we remained for several days. I'd never been in New England, and even though I'd not left the base, I admired the trees and towns and steepled churches from the air as we let down toward the field.

Later, as we climbed from the Manchester runway during our departure, we suddenly became aware of tree-covered hills directly in our path. They grew quickly! With a ridiculous mental gesture I tried to lift the airplane with the force of my will, my muscles straining to bring it up. Under full power we skimmed over the trees, every leaf and twig sharp and clear from my position in the Plexiglas nose. We flew north from Manchester on our way to Gander, Newfoundland, passing over magical places like

5

Moncton, New Brunswick and Prince Edward Island. I looked down longingly on the island with its greenness, bays, villages and roads, and had vowed that I would travel there someday.

We were grounded several days at Gander because of bad weather over the North Atlantic, giving us some free time. The cooks at the mess hall told us that if we should catch any fish in the lake nearby, they would cook them for us. We borrowed fishing gear and walked along a muddy path strewn with fir needles until we reached the shore, the sky over us a brilliant blue, the slender trees around us a dark forest green. Near a weathered fallen log we cast our lines into the pristine water, simply enjoying the quietness and beauty of the place, not really caring whether we caught any fish or not. After an hour of patient trying, we gave up without ever feeling a bite on our lines, but the idle time afforded a pleasant diversion from our thoughts of what lay ahead.

* * *

Suddenly, the heavy thumping of shoes on the stairway breaks the silence of the barracks. A strained voice, sounding as though someone carries a heavy load says, "Come on Podoske! Let's get up these stairs. Come on!"

As the door bursts open, Warren and Johnston, with their arms firmly locked around Podoske's arms and shoulders, explode into the room. A thick wave of Podoske's hair tumbles down his forehead, his hat perched on his head at a wild angle. An impish grin breaks out on his face. Johnston, his always-glistening cheeks and forehead beaming with the flush of the cold wind and bourbon, says, "Okay Podoske. We got you here, and you're gonna stay here. You understand!"

Johnston turns to me, still out of breath from urging him up the stairs.

"You know what this crazy guy was doing? He was so looped that he was down near the nurses' quarters trying to get one of them to go out with him."

Warren, his speech animated with alcohol, warns Podoske about getting into trouble if he bothers the nurses.

"Stevens," says Johnston, "we're going out again, but he's gotta stay here. Watch him, and don't let him leave the room or he's liable to get in trouble. Do anything. Hit 'im if you have to, or knock 'im out, but don't let him go."

"I'll watch him the best I can."

Podoske crawls up on the top bunk, stretching as though he wants to nap. Johnston and Warren, a trifle unsteady on their feet, shuffle out the door, imploring me once more to be sure and keep him in the room.

He doesn't plan to sleep as I had hoped. He lies on the top bunk, cradling his head in one hand as he leans on his elbow and looks out at me with that same devilish expression.

"I'm gonna go back there," he says, his grin transformed into a mocking smile.

"You better stay here, Podoske. If you go out there you'll be in trouble for sure.

"As soon as Warren and Johnson get far enough away, I'm goin' back to the nurses headquarters."

"Come on, Podoske, stay here with me. Don't take a chance and go back there," I plead.

We banter back and forth for nearly ten minutes before he sits up on the bunk, dangling his legs over the side.

"You don't understand anything, Stevens. You don't know anything about it."

He quickly slides down from the bunk, brushes by me, bolts through the door.

I am powerless to stop him. My weak appeals are no match for his bourbon-induced passion and determination. He's right. I don't understand anything or know anything about it, neither the intensity of his drive nor the alcoholic release of inhibitions that allows a man to fly freely with his instincts.

I feel rotten that I'd lacked the strength to stop him, and might be responsible for the trouble that probably lies ahead. I know that Johnston and Warren will be angry with me for letting him go, but how was I to stop him? I couldn't hit him as Johnston had suggested. How could I slug a friend? Anyone? As an adult I'd never struck anyone out of anger or frustration. It just wasn't in me. I'd never been mad enough. In a practical sense, Podoske outweighed me by 40 or 50 pounds and enjoyed a much more solid build.

It seems to me that everyone except me is drunk. Perhaps as soon as tomorrow evening each crew will fly out alone across the North Atlantic to

England and then shortly into combat. That's what it's all about. Bourbon and diversion make it easier to look upon the cold face of death. I think about England as I lie on my bunk, but the only visions that well up in my mind are the newsreel films of London's fiery destruction in the German bombing raids. I imagine myself walking down a street there with the rubble of buildings all around me. I am about to match those scenes with what I can see with my own eyes.

Barging into the darkness of the room, flipping on the light, the three of them return nearly an hour later.

"Hey Stevens," says Johnston, "I thought you were going to keep Podoske in the room. We found him right down there by the nurses again."

"I'm sorry. I tried my best to keep him here."

They all breathe heavily and clumsily as they take off their uniforms. This time they're ready for bed, and I'm relieved. At last the lights go out.

"Oh God," moans Johnston, "my bed's in a tail spin, and I can't bring it out." We snicker, but quickly lapse into the rhythmic breathing of sleep.

THE CROSSING

Bringing our plane slowly around to the correct compass heading, Johnston points it up into the cave-like void of night, a scattering of stars providing our only light. In spite of the risks facing our untried crew and the specter of the unknown lurking in the darkness, we're buoyed by a spirit of optimism and the excitement of ferrying a bomber across the Atlantic. We have so much confidence in Johnston and Podoske as pilots that once aloft we give little thought to what might happen should our engines falter, or worse, should we have to ditch our plane in the cold water.

I'm useless as a navigator tonight as pilotage is impossible over a dark ocean where no cities spread their phosphorescent glows on the horizon, and no light patterns outline the turn of a river or the runways of an airport. We have only two methods of knowing where we are, Warren's celestial navigation and the powerful radio beam from Prestwick in Scotland. Warren stands with his sextant at the astro-bubble, already taking fixes on the stars while I help him time his readings.

Earlier in the day the weather had finally cleared at Gander, giving some of us the chance to fly the northern route to the British Isles. We loaded all of our belongings, checked with meteorology about winds and weather fronts en route and made sure that we had enough fuel for the distance. We had flown at night many times, but never so far and over so much open water where emergency landings would be impossible. A sense of adventure, of attempting a flight of this magnitude for the first time, thrills us just enough to subdue our tensions.

Once out over the Atlantic, suspended in the blackness and the steady drone of our engines, we settle in for the long trip ahead. I've no intention of sleeping as I want to know approximately where we are at all times. I want to be a part of our getting there. Johnston reports that he has a radio fix on Prestwick, and that we seem to be on course. The factory-new Boeing B-17 flies smoothly, each part performing perfectly. Every mile we fly gives us more confidence.

The intercom is quiet, the only sounds being the all-enveloping energy of our four engines, metallic vibrations in our navigator's and bombardier's compartments and the air rushing past the nose. Instrument dials and the tips of switches glow in the dark. Warren stands in the compartment again, his head and sextant poked up into the Plexiglas dome, searching the sky for a recognizable star. The chill of the night seeps in, but our fleece-lined leather flying suits keep us reasonably warm. With the fix taken, Warren and I huddle over the navigator's table, a small light shining on his calculations, our eyes peering at each other over our oxygen masks.

The flight is long, almost tedious except for the persistent stimulation of wondering exactly where we are and looking out at the magnificence of the heavens. At times I sit in the bombardier's seat just gazing out at it all, a horizonless bowl of night speckled with stars. I look deep into the universe and wonder about myself. I'm nineteen years old, and every moment that passes brings me closer to combat, a business that I know little about. I'm not an aggressive man. I've never hurt anyone in my life that I know of, and I don't hate anybody, yet I'm on my way to inflict damage on the enemy, a flagrantly aggressive act, and for that they will rightfully attempt to kill me.

Following our course with Warren takes my thoughts away from myself, away from the lonely strangeness of the night. We confer over the maps, marking our assumed position—our place on the earth at this moment.

Halfway through the 10-hour flight our plane flutters as we enter the murkiness of a weather front. For a moment Johnston switches on the landing lights. Snowflakes stream toward us like armies of moths in the beam. We have lost the stars, our only key to how far we have progressed along our route. In the cockpit Johnston reports that the plane is increasingly difficult to handle. Out in the freezing night a film of ice builds up on the leading edges of our wings, affecting lift and the control surfaces.

"Pilot to navigator and bombardier."

"Go ahead."

"Don't wake anybody up, but the damn plane's acting a bit sluggish. I have to work at maintaining our altitude. I think we're okay, but I thought I'd let you know."

"Roger."

We can't turn back as we've passed the point of no return. We must go on in spite of the icing.

He employs the deicing boots, rods that move under rubber on the leading edges of the wings, to crack the glaze.

Most of the crew sleeps, unaware that there is any problem, the pilot, co-pilot and Lucas, the engineer, bearing the concern and tension of keeping the plane flying. The boots sluff off the ice, but it continually forms, the supercooled cloud droplets freezing on contact with the wings. Warren and I, trying to keep track of our position, understand the problem, but have confidence that Johnston will solve it. I think about the dark cold, inhospitable sea beneath us, a scene that we can only imagine—ink-black swells and icy water, fish darting through the midnight sea. We pass over it all in our aluminum cocoon, separated from it and the arctic temperatures of the altitude, but our shelter is in trouble.

We finally break out of the clouds into the starry night, again listening to the comfortable monotony of our engines and the subtle beating of our own hearts. The radio beam from Prestwick that had been wide and weak earlier has now narrowed, and is stronger. The plane handles well again, and we're on course, but we're not sure about how far along it we've flown.

Shortly before dawn we pick up the radio signal from Shannon, Ireland, our possible landing point. The first dull fluorescent blue of dawn glows softly on the leading edges of our wings, and reveals a solid deck of lower clouds beneath us, a blue-gray mattress of fluff. By the time the blood-red smear of dawn washes the eastern horizon, we calculate that we must be near the Irish coast.

"Pilot to navigator."

"Go ahead."

"We must be about there. Don't you think so?"

"Yeah, this should be about right."

"We'll go down beneath the soup and see what we can see."

Swallowed by pearly translucence, our wing tips nearly invisible, we wait to burst out into what we hope is the clear air beneath. Ice crystals form on and around the navigator's machine guns, but the wings appear to be all right. Blinded by the thick vapor, we all hang in suspense, wondering what we'll see when we emerge.

Once we poke through the low base of the stratus, a lively sea appears beneath us, and several miles ahead, the slate-colored outline of what we believe to be the Irish coast, its highest peaks lost in mist. Flying at a lower altitude, we speed over the coast, the waves collapsing into wild white foam against its cliffs and rocks. A narrow country road winds near a dark-roofed stone house and through the deepest green velvety hills I have ever known. Satisfied that we have really found Ireland, we radio the Shannon tower. They tell us that their airport is crowded, and so is the field at Prestwick, Scotland. They order us on to Valley, Wales, a disappointment, as we're weary from the long hours and tension of the trip and are ready to land. We had also hoped to look at Ireland from the ground.

Climbing to a higher altitude, back up through the overcast, we head eastward toward the British Isles. By the time we reach the Welsh airstrip, the sun shines brightly. Even though I'm exhausted from the lack of sleep, I'm amazed at what I see below—the geometric patchwork of fields, the small curved roads, scraps of forests, sheep grazing in lush green pastures. We are close to the ground now, only a few feet lying between us and the completion of the trip. Johnston, who usually lands the plane smoothly, pounds the wheels into the runway. With a painful shudder the plane bounces once then settles into a gentle roll.

Once on the ground, the plane parked and the tired engines and propellers still at last, I ask Johnston, "Who made that landing anyway, Podoske?"

A half-smile spreads over his weary face as he answers, "No, I landed it. I was just tired."

He had had the ultimate responsibility for the success of the flight, most of the burden resting on his shoulders. He's clearly drained. I respect him as a pilot so much that I would never criticize him, or Podoske either, about their flying.

Our feet now tread British soil, a fact that, coupled with my heavy-eyed drowsiness, seems strangely dreamlike and ethereal.

THE INTERIM

Gliding by almost silently except for the muffled clanking of the locomotive's driving rods, a short freight train whispers by the hedge- rows near the edge of the airfield. With its small boxcars, each with only four wheels, the train symbolizes my first impression of the British Isles—that everything seems smaller and quieter than its counterpart in America. A few Lilliputian automobiles roll over ribbon-narrow roads that loop and wind over miles of small green hills. The English live in modest houses with steeply pitched roofs and ride plain bicycles with slender tires and hand brakes. It is a quaint and curious country, the sights strangely resembling the illustrations that I remember from the fairy tale books I had read as a child.

Since the airstrip at Valley has only token facilities for housing airmen, trucks transport us and several other crews to the nearest railroad station where we wait for a train that will whisk us off to a staging area in England. It arrives in a flurry of clanging, hissing and escaping steam. Once aboard, Podoske, Warren, Johnston and I sit in a compartment with two bench-like seats facing each other, an arrangement quite new to us. Sitting across from us is a middle-aged British officer, a portly man with balding hair and a walrus moustache. Two rows of colorful campaign ribbons stretch across his uniform. Perhaps seeing that we are young and inexperienced at war, and apparently feeling superior because of his vast experience, he begins to speak to us, his voice reminding me of character actors I'd seen in British films.

"I've been in three wars," he announces in his gravelly voice. "I've been in the Boer War, the first World War, and now this one."

Searching our faces with his light blue eyes, he appears to be waiting for a response. Receiving none, he finally says with a half-smile beneath his moustache, a twinkle in his eye, "Extraordinary, don't you think?" We politely agree, but at the same time wince at what in America would be bragging. I'm sure he expects us to be curious about his war adventures, but I really don't know what to ask him. About to go into combat myself, I don't feel much like listening to his tales anyway.

Warming up to us, he begins to tell us jokes, none of which I understand. The punch lines, if there are any, escape me. The others, seeming as confused as I am, see nothing funny in them either. When I think he's finished telling one, I try to chuckle only out of politeness. I don't know whether the man is at fault or that British humor is simply different from American. Funniest is the man himself, this strange old fellow who attempts to entertain us with his puzzling witticisms. I find myself wondering what his duties are in this third war of his.

I'm much more interested in looking out the window at the countryside. Deep green fields, flocks of grazing sheep, quiet mirror-like rivers and thick hedgerows captivate me. I watch villages fly by with their stone houses, churches and vegetable plots, and towns with rows of flats all joining one another like a great brick wall with gables, doors and windows.

When the train stops at a station, I jump off in search of something to eat. I walk into the congested terminal, bumping my way through the crowds to a small stand where a middle-aged woman sells what appear to be small pies, about the size of muffins. I reach out to her with my coins, and she hands me one of them. I expect it to be warm, but it feels cold in my hand. Without knowing what's inside, I hungrily bite into it. Looking down at the place where I had just bitten, I see only a kind of foggy gelatin filling with bits of fish suspended in it. I'm so hungry that I devour it anyway, actually relishing its unusual flavor.

As I stand on the platform, a fish train slowly rumbles through the station laying down an invisible smoke screen of stench. The small box-cars appear weathered and pathetic under the dull sky. I also make the mistake of using a public toilet on the platform. Its acrid odor extends beyond the open door, nearly overpowering me as I enter. I breathe through my mouth only, trying to spare my nose. The WC hadn't been cleaned in years, maybe never. A patina of brown crystallized urine covers the urinal, a sight that nearly gags me.

Back on the train again, I realize that as quaint and as beautiful as everything looks out of the train window, certain parts of the English scene don't stand up under closer scrutiny.

* * *

The staging area, a city of barracks built out in the country, teems with new crews, all trained in the United States and as ready as they will ever be to be parceled out to the various bomber groups scattered all over East Central England. Our primary purpose, while we wait for assignment, is to learn how to operate an ingenious British navigation instrument called the G-box, a small console with a cathode ray tube that traces green lines on its screen. When a navigator flying over the continent tunes in several fixed radio points in England, its quivering blips will indicate his exact position. Since each bomber is equipped with one, it might be possible for a plane, separated from its group or off course, to find its way home. It could save our lives one day. We spend hours watching the bright chartreuse squiggles on the screen, trying to match them up to determine simulated imaginary positions.

Shortly after we arrive at the staging area, the long-awaited invasion of Normandy begins, D-day. Squadrons of American medium attack bombers, Douglas A-20s and Martin B-26s, roar over our barracks in their never-ending shuttles to the French coast to assist the landing troops. An excitement ripples through the camp. This is the first step in ending the war. We know that the operation will be difficult, and that in some manner all of us will be involved—and soon.

* * *

Finally assigned to the 351st Bomb Group at Polebrook, our crew along with several others once more speeds through the English countryside on a train, this time to reach our new base. According to our orders, we have several changes to make at cities unfamiliar to us. Arriving at the first transfer point, we must wait for over an hour for our next train. A group of us, having nothing better to do, mill around the station, step over the sidetracks and enjoy the sunshine. As we stand among the switches, talking to each other, the station agent approaches, stepping over the rails as he nears us.

"I say", he says in a pleasant voice, "could you help me move this carriage over to the other side track there?"

When we realize that by "carriage" he means the passenger coach poised on the track near us, we look at him in disbelief.

"Come on," he says, "we'll just push it."

The car appears so formidable that we think only a locomotive capable of budging it. The agent releases the hand brake, and tells us all to push from one end. Surprisingly, with little effort, the car rolls quite easily. He throws a switch, and with a number of us still shoving on the other end of the car, we urge it on to the proper siding. Used to American bigness and massiveness, we are amazed at how easy the relatively delicate coach is to move.

We wait again at our next transfer point, this time a larger station with several raised platforms. We shuffle around on one of them, just watching people and absorbing the novelty of its Victorian architecture.

Suddenly a uniformed man struts out, blowing a small whistle.

"Everyone stand back please! Everyone stand back!" he yells as he blows several more shrill warnings.

Waiting passengers obediently back away from the track as the red nose of a speeding locomotive charges through the station, smoke and steam laying back from its stack, its falsetto whistle shrieking a final warning. It rips through the station, its driving rods a blur, its cars merely a quick flickering clicking, its swift passing churning a wind that scatters dust, and whips the clothes of the waiting passengers. Then it disappears down the track in a haze of sooty smoke.

The speed of English trains impresses me, but I chuckle at the locomotive's high-pitched whistle, so "tea kettle-like" compared to the deep melodious tones of American locomotives. I had never seen a train rush through a station like that in America.

Our last rail journey takes us toward Peterborough where trucks will transport us to the airport at Polebrook, home of the 351st Bomb Group. I'm curious about what lies ahead for us at the airfield. Nervously excited at the prospect of new adventures, I'm also apprehensive about the unknown. We race across the English fields and through the hills on our way to that final point. I'm about to realize the grim climax of all of my training—induction, classification, preflight courses, gunnery school, bombardier instruction, crew training and now assignment to a combat squadron. The preparation had all taken such a short time. I had walked down that windy hill in San

Pedro in my civilian clothes at Fort MacArthur just slightly over a year ago, and now I'm on my way to an operational base where real bomber crews fly real missions over enemy territory.

POLEBROOK

Arriving at a new base is always the same. Buildings and roads, barracks and hangars all shimmer in the dream-like light of their strangeness. A new person feels lost, as though he's been suddenly set down in an unfamiliar neighborhood, an interloper.

Although the air base at Polebrook is to be our home, we feel more out of place than ever. Not only are the surroundings new to us, but so are the men, veterans who have seen combat, have endured enemy fire and have seen their friends shot down. A few display ribbons on their tunics representing medals they've earned. Some wear rumpled, soiled hats, and strut around with leather A-2 jackets with the names of their planes and painted rows of bombs on their backs showing how many missions they'd survived. Even though we appreciate and honor the men, they also intimidate us.

Johnston, Warren, Podoske and I walk along the curb of the main road leading through the base looking for our assigned barracks. The sound of a revving engine drifts in from the hangar area, and the faint smell of coal smoke lingers in the air. Feeling overwhelmed by the strange place, we become tense, even a trifle grim.

Finally I say," Well, we've found the base personnel office and the base headquarters, now I wonder where the base shithouse is?"

Johnston begins to laugh and says, "I wondered when you were going to come up with something, Stevens."

23

Podoske and Warren chuckle too, the laughing relaxing the tension that had stiffened us all. We crack more nervous jokes with each other as we shuffle along through the drab barracks, looking for ours.

As we walk, we can see some B-17s near the repair hangars and others scattered at a distance around the field on their individual hardstands. All of them bear a black triangle with a white "J" inscribed within it and a broad diagonal red stripe, both on the tail, the special symbol of the 351st Bomb Group.

We pass several groups of "bungalows" and Nissen huts before we arrive at our dull-looking quarters. We push through the door and peer down the length of it to the single coal stove, its large black vent pipe running up through the ceiling. Down each side of the barracks small beds rest in neat rows, plenty of sleeping room for the officers of about a dozen crews. Showers and toilets are outside in the back.

Except for two men in suntan uniforms, the room is empty. We edge in to search for our beds. We find them but can't help wondering about the crew that occupied them before us, whether they had simply completed their missions or had been shot down. As we stand in the aisle between the beds, the two men sidle up to me.

One of them, a slender, sandy-haired lieutenant, asks in a serious voice, "Say, what size shirt do you wear?"

"Why? Why do you want to know?" "Well if or when you go down, will you let me have your shirts? I think they'll fit me just right."

"By the way", the other man chimes in, "you don't happen to have a bicycle do you? I could really use one. If anything should happen to you, will you give it to me?"

My excitement, even my nervous levity dissolves under their insensitivity. Instead of welcoming me to the squadron, they attempt to have fun with me by heightening the apprehensions that I already have. Certain kinds of men find great pleasure in hazing the uninitiated.

At dinnertime we walk the short distance to the mess hall where we're again reminded of our inexperience. Stenciled along one wall is a long record of all of the previous missions flown by the 351st, listing the target and the date of the raid, each within the outlines of huge black bombs. Since it had been one of the first groups to operate from England, the list is extensive. So much history had gone on before us, and now we are about to be injected into it. But for now we can only sit at the long tables eating our supper, and looking at the wall, knowing very little about what those men had experienced.

* * *

As we train at the base, and become acquainted with more members of our squadron, good men all varying in the number of missions they had flown, we begin to relax. Our dream-like trance fades away, and we begin to feel a part of the 351st.

Training flights in formation flying and the methods of assembling with other planes for missions familiarizes me with the special look of the English countryside below. The roads are seldom straight, and the fields resemble a chaotic green mosaic that sometimes bends with a river or road or follows the contours of the gentle hills. Scattered through it all are scraps of forests, their geometric outlines useful in determining our position as their exact shapes are featured on our detailed maps. The land contrasts sharply with the vast flatness, long straight roads and quilt-like arrays of farms and fields in America, especially with the parched, brush-stippled plains of Texas where we had received so much of our early training.

One flight takes us over Coventry, the city that had been devastated earlier by German bombers. When we'd traveled through the pastoral countryside on trains, I'd seen no war damage, but looking down on Coventry represents a totally different sight, one that changes my entire outlook. Even though much of the debris had been removed after the raids, the city still appears like a huge graveyard of hazy gray rubble. Indistinct patterns of streets run through the broken city, the buildings with their roofs and most of their walls blown away resembling photographs I had seen of the ruins of ancient cities. I watch it all pass slowly under the Plexiglas nose of our bomber, sobered by the stark picture of raw war.

Our brief preparation is over. We are ready to be called for our first mission. I sit in the dim light of the barracks, writing a letter home. I had finally received a few letters and feel relieved that the communication lines are opening at last. I stop writing, and use a GI handkerchief, a pesky cold having descended on me since the moment we'd landed in England. I struggle with the letter as I don't have much energy and can't write about any details because of military restrictions.

The strains of organ music drift over from a radio at the other end of the barracks. I think about being home in church, safe, sound and protected, far away from the prospect of the sinister unknowns that lie ahead of us.

LE BOURGET—THE FIRST MISSION

Sounding as though it had suddenly materialized out of my own dreams, the sergeant's harsh voice shatters the peaceful darkness of the barracks. I'm warm and comfortable, lost in the soft-breathing innocence of sleep when he flicks on the barracks light and begins to shout out the names of the men who will fly today's mission. I hope my name isn't read. All I want to do is roll on my side, pull the covers up over my eyes and continue sleeping. It's only three o'clock in the morning.

Some of the men whose names have been called sit up in bed or struggle out of their blankets, their eyes puffed and blinking, their hair blown and twisted into unruly tangles by the winds of sleep.

"Johnston, Podoske, Warren, Stevens," yells the sergeant.

The calling of my name washes over me like an electric wave, then ebbs away just as quickly. Podoske, hearing his, rises on one elbow, his thick brown hair in disarray. As is his habit, he reaches under his pillow for his pack of cigarettes. A wreath of bluish smoke swirls about his head as he sits on the edge of his bed, spitting out loose shreds of tobacco clinging to his lips.

Our crew has never been on a bombing mission. We know little about what to expect except for the chilling accounts of the experienced men in our barracks. We'd also been exposed to a parade of wartime Hollywood movies and newsreels as well as numerous training films viewed in the safety of our classrooms in Texas and Louisiana. But how accurate were they?

Most of us are quiet, uttering only a few muffled words to each other. Still hazy with sleep and inwardly anxious about what might lie ahead, I stand silently with the other men in the latrine, shaving closely so that my oxygen mask will fit snugly, the sweet scents of creams, soaps and lotions gradually replacing the room's dankness. I look at my face in the mirror and think about the mission ahead, our target for today still unknown.

By the time we reach the briefing room, we're livelier, but there's no levity. We sit among a subdued babble of voices, our eyes directed toward a small stage where closed curtains conceal the great map that holds the plan for today's mission. Curious and concerned about what lies behind them, we wait anxiously for their opening.

Suddenly the briefing officer struts through the room from behind us.

"Tench-hut! "yells an orderly.

We rise, and stand at attention until he reaches the front.

"At ease, men," he says severely.

We sit, relieved that we're finally about to know where we'll fly. After a few brief words, he pulls the cord, and the curtains part. Red yarn stretches from point to point on the huge map, marking our flight path to the target and back to England. It all looks very neat and well planned, the precise crimson geometry of it imprinted over the curved coastline, winding rivers and towns of France. Our targets are the runways and hangers at Le Bourget Airfield just outside of Paris.

The men's faces are set, even grim, as we listen to the details of the mission. We all know that any target near the French capital will be well defended. Although we listen carefully to the specifics of the mission, I imagine each man, like me, privately wonders about his chances. I don't fully understand that as yet, but I read it in the faces of the veterans.

The mission explained and our hack watches set exactly on the same time, we shuffle out into the darkness, most of us heading to the mess hall. I walk in a fuzzy medium of unreality, all of our movements dream-like in the dewy blackness of the early morning. Even though apprehensive, I devour a breakfast of eggs, bacon and fried potatoes.

Afterwards Warren, the navigator, and I walk down to the armament shack to pick up the "innards" of the machine guns for the chin turret and the navigator's swivels. Sleepy-eyed armament men in green fatigues check them out to us and mark their records. The shack smells of machine oil and steel, the clicking of metal and the somber voices of gunners resounding throughout the dimly lit room. With our heavy weapons clasped in our arms, we wait outside in the dark for a truck to take us out to the planes. It's cumbersome climbing into it wearing our electrically heated suits, flying suits, parachute harnesses and Mae Wests.

The damp chill of the morning washes over us as we drive toward the scattered hardstands where our bombers wait. Subdued lighting around our plane gives us just enough illumination to complete our preflight tasks. I load my guns into the chin turret then pull myself up through the escape hatch into the nose, into the familiar fragrance of rubber, plastic, oil and aluminum.

By the time Johnston fires up the engines, each one whining and spewing smoke as it springs to life, the first light of dawn shows gray-blue on the eastern horizon. The crew chief pulls the chocks, and with a flourish of his hand he bids us goodbye. We wheel around then roll slowly along the taxi strip toward the runway, joining other bombers that follow each other in a long shadowy row.

At the head of the runway, we wait for the signal to take off, our engines roaring, our plane quivering behind its set brakes. With full power, the brakes released, we surge down the runway, slowly at first, but gradually gaining speed. We have never taken off with a full load of fuel and three tons of bombs before. The Flying Fortress struggles down the runway, the air speed indicator needle moving up only slowly. In the nose I watch my own dial and look ahead to the dusky end of the runway, wondering about how much space we have left. The needle creeps above 100 mph, then towards the 130 mph that we need for takeoff. With little runway left Johnston finally lifts the plane, folding the wheels as we streak out over the dim green fields and hedgerows.

Climbing steadily, we bank gently to the right, heading toward the northwest, the engines laboring. As we gain altitude the dark shapes of other bombers trail out ahead of us. The tiny silhouettes of still others from different fields appear far in the distance. My chest pack parachute rests on the floor beside me with my steel helmet and flak jackets.

At Melton Mowbray we bank to the left toward Birmingham, still ascending. After another left turn we head south, and begin to assemble with other planes from our group around the Deenethorpe buncher. The lead plane fires shots straight up with a Very pistol, the two small yellow and red fireballs rising into the morning sky, then falling in trails of smoke as they gradually burn out. Each group fires its own colors, making it easier for pilots to find their own. As we are up above 10,000 feet, I strap on my oxygen mask and plug in my electrically heated suit.

The planes gradually gather, assume their assigned places in their formation. Groups merge into combat wings, and hundreds of us, with planes stretching out ahead as far as I can see, like orderly swarms of locusts, begin the journey to France. By the time we reach the English coast at Selsey Bill near Portsmouth, we fly at 18,000 feet.

Once out over the English Channel, I reconnect my oxygen hose to a small portable tank, then struggle past the navigator, up through the space between and behind the pilots, past the engineer and top turret to the bomb bay. On the narrow catwalk I look at our lethal load, twelve 500-pound bombs painted dull olive drab with two bands of yellow around them, one at the tip and one near the tail. I touch their hard bodies, feeling the chill of them through my gloves. One by one I pull the tagged pins from the fuzes of each of the twelve bombs, stuffing the pins into the pocket of my flying suit.

Back up in the nose I fire several rounds from the twin machine-guns in my chin turret, their staccato vibrations assuring me that the cartridge belts are feeding and firing properly. We climb over the channel, reaching 23,000 feet by the time we pass over the French coast. I pull my steel helmet down over my leather one, and slip into my heavy flak vests, overlapping metal strips covered with corduroy. I lay another flak vest between my legs as special protection for what the crews call "the family jewels." There must be sons and daughters in our lives, in some hazy faraway time. I briefly think about Le Bourget Airfield where Lindberg had landed after his trans-Atlantic adventure, about our own similar flight in ferrying our plane and the subtle irony of bombing that particular airfield on our first raid.

Soon after passing into France we begin to bear to the east toward Paris. Long before we reach the target sporadic antiaircraft fire appears ahead of us, a chance hit, knocking down one of the B-17s. It falls straight down like a chunk of inert metal, tumbling slowly end over end, like a toy airplane dropped off of a high bridge by a mischievous child. It accelerates, plummeting down toward the hazy gray fields below. I see no parachutes. It drops so quickly that I think it impossible for anyone to escape. Behind my mask my mouth is open in silent awe as I watch it. Finally I can't see it any more.

I think about the men inside, all of them rousted out of their warm beds only hours ago, just as I had been. They too had shaved in their latrines and attended briefing, and now they are gone. It could have been me. The vision of the falling plane repeats itself over and over in my mind.

In the movies and newsreels planes that were shot down were supposed to spiral earthward trailing streams of black smoke and wailing like old coffee grinders. This plane had fallen straight down in utter silence, the droning of our own engines the only audible sound.

We bank in a wide circle then fly toward the target where a dark, smoky pall of merged antiaircraft bursts lies ahead of us.

As we approach, the death-black smear of smoke resolves itself into individual specks, then blooming blossoms as the flak begins to burst all around us. Strangely, the flak is "silent" too. The bursts resemble dark hourglasses that angrily twist and boil into amorphous shapes. I catch myself unconsciously leaning away from it, as though that would somehow protect me. I mutter what I remember of the twenty-third Psalm—"yea though I walk through the valley of the shadow of death."

An excited voice pierces the intercom, "Tail gunner to pilot. They got one plane from the group behind us. He's goin' down!"

Johnston calmly replies, "Okay. Let's reserve the intercom for emergencies."

I check my intervalometer and switches, keeping my eye on the lead plane. When that bombardier drops his bombs, I must instantly drop mine.

He opens his bomb bay doors. Quickly I open mine.

"Radio operator to bombardier. Bomb bay doors opening," yells Witherspoon over the intercom.

From his radio compartment he peeks into the bays through his small door.

"Bomb bay doors all the way open!" he screams in a shrill agitated voice.

Satisfied, I place my hand by the release switch, waiting for the lead plane's bombs to drop.

"Tail gunner hit! Tail gunner hit!" shouts Stanowick into the intercom.

Softly and silently the bombs begin to fall out of the lead plane. I immediately hit the switch, but nothing happens! My indicator lights show that all my bombs are still in their racks.

"What the hell's the matter?" screams Johnston.

"I don't know," I say sheepishly. "They just won't release. Some sort of malfunction."

"Okay. Close the bomb bay doors," says Johnston, clearly irritated.

"Tail gunner to pilot. I'm okay. I'm not hit. A chunk of flak punched a hole in my window, but it missed me."

Just after the bomb run, one of our planes in the formation ahead suddenly lights up like a gigantic dandelion flower, having taken a direct hit. Pieces of it fall to earth. I had never realized that a plane could disintegrate so quickly, could disappear in a flash. I swallow hard and think about the men, whether they had even had time to know what had happened to them. I glance at my parachute beside me on the floor. If I were to be similarly blown out, I wouldn't have had my parachute. I pick up the clumsy chest pack which feels like a loaf of heavy bread, and hook it over one ring of my harness.

As we head northwest out of the target area, we finally escape the barrage. Miraculously none of our crew is injured, and all four engines churn. I can't understand why my bombs hadn't released. Perhaps there'd been an electrical failure or icing in the system. I feel that I'd done everything correctly, but I begin to doubt myself. We'll have to land now with a full load of bombs, and I'm sure that Johnston is not going to like it. Confidence and doubt chase each other around in my mind.

As we cross back over the English Channel, feeling the blessed euphoria of safety, I again make my way to the bomb bay. I look at my unruly bombs hanging there in the shadows, mocking me. Why didn't they release? Working carefully, I reinsert the pins in each fuze for absolute safety when we land. Having let down to 12,000 feet, we re-enter England over Beachy Head, landing at Polebrook shortly after 11 a.m., slightly over six hours from the time we'd taken off.

Soon after landing, we gather for debriefing. The crews, although tired and pale, babble about what they'd seen and what had happened to them. On a table rest dozens of shot glasses filled with amber bourbon, one for each flyer to steady his nerves. Our crew sits down with one of the intelligence officers to answer questions, and describe anything we had observed that might be of significance—where antiaircraft fire had occurred, its intensity, the spotting of enemy interceptor planes, anything unusual on the ground.

Johnston, Warren and Podoske sip their bourbon as we talk to the intelligence officer, but I have none.

"Hey, Stevens," says Podoske, "next time take yours, then give it to me, will ya."

"Yeah. Okay, I will from now on."

None of the crew says anything to me about our bombs not dropping. I interpret their silence as a vote of confidence. I'd never had any problem bombing before, so all are convinced with me that some sort of malfunction had taken place.

Famished, we troop to the mess hall for a late lunch. At least one of the missions stenciled on its walls, when it was put up, would be ours.

I stand in the shower, letting its pure warm water run over my body, cleansing it of sweat and tension. Several other men do the same, and talk about the mission.

"Did you hear about our squadrons that flew with the other wing? Three of them were knocked out of formation by flak. Two might have ditched in the channel, but one somehow made it back to England."

My eyeballs feel strange, like large hard marbles holding my eyes open wide. I hope the "bulging" is not visible to the other men. Perhaps my eyes are glazed, but I don't feel frightened. I'm exhausted. Possibly the pressure of fatigue inflates my eyes. All I can think about is slipping into bed.

Word comes through to me that the mechanics have checked our plane and have found nothing wrong with the bomb release mechanism. They further state that I was at fault because I hadn't opened the bomb bay doors fully which would have prevented the bombs from releasing. How do they know how far the bomb bay doors had been opened? I think to myself. I know when the doors are open fully and when they're not.

Sure, the mechanisms may work beautifully on the ground, but at the low temperatures of high altitude conditions are different. At first I defend myself to myself, then I worry that the mechanics might be correct. Perhaps the doors had just been a few millimeters from being fully open. Or maybe a mechanic had covered up his own mistakes by blaming me.

I agonize over what I might have done. Perhaps in the excitement of the bomb run I had overlooked something. I may have jeopardized the lives of ten men, all of them risking their skins for just one reason, to place our bombs on the hangars and runways of the Le Bourget Airport, and I had failed them.

At the same time I know I've been trained well, and I'm confident of my skills. I gradually fall asleep in the same bed I'd struggled out of so early in the morning, without my problem being resolved.

BACK TO FRANCE—ANGOULEME

Still weary from yesterday's mission to Le Bourget, I again suffer the shouts of the unsympathetic orderlies as they jolt me awake long before dawn. Now that I know what to expect on a mission, the cold electric wave that washes over me as they read my name is like the impact of an unseen breaker, the kind that used to tumble me roughly into the wet sand when I was a child. Just as I did then, I simply get up on my feet again. With a dull aching in my bones, I quietly dress.

When the colonel pulls the curtains at briefing, our eyes follow the long doglegged stretch of red yarn down into west central France, not far from Bordeaux, another long mission. Our targets are the marshalling yards and roundhouse at Angouleme where Intelligence claims that one train carrying a German Panzer Division has stopped. Since our route carefully avoids most known heavily defended areas, we're not expected to encounter much opposition.

We take off at 0400, the sky barely light. Our bomber's belly carries twelve 500-pound general-purpose bombs, enough in themselves to create havoc in the railroad yards. I have been told ahead of time that the regular release mechanism on this particular plane, an old battle-weary one, is inoperative, and that I must salvo the bombs, let them go all at once with a mechanical lever. I've neither salvoed a load before nor have I seen a device exactly like this one, but its operation appears to be simple enough.

Having assembled at 13,000 feet, we head southward like orderly flocks of geese, leaving the English coast at Selsey Bill near Portsmouth. Out over the channel we climb to 20,000 feet, the coast of France out ahead of us. I think about my position in the nose with its Plexiglas windows, a special bay from which I can look out over hundreds of square miles. It is like a greenhouse and about as safe. I had a spectacular view of the madness of yesterday's mission from my glassy perch, visions I see yet and probably always will.

We cross into France over the north-facing beaches east of the Cherbourg Peninsula. Taking no chances, I protect myself with my steel helmet and flak jackets, attach my chest pack to one ring of my parachute harness. We fly deep into the Continent, but as yet the German antiaircraft guns, which are probably out of range, remain silent, and the Luftwaffe has stayed away from us. Our P-47 Thunderbolt escort discourages their interceptors. They'll leave us soon, but P-51 Mustangs will replace them to protect us over the target.

After flying for nearly two hours over France without seeing a single burst of flak, we turn toward the target at Angouleme. Even though the Germans had not fired upon us, the tension of thinking they might at any moment is always with us.

"Pilot to bombardier," says Johnston over the intercom. "If that salvo lever doesn't release the bombs, tell me immediately, and I'll drop them with the emergency switch I have up here."

"Okay, but I don't think I'll have any trouble. Looks simple enough to me."

All I have to do is pull it. I don't even have to set up the intervalometer that regulates the spacing of the bombs on the ground. I look at the red lever again and feel confident that all is well.

The marshalling yard, not important enough for the Germans to protect, lies in front of us. We begin the bomb run, not sighting any flak as yet. The lead plane opens its bomb bay doors, and I immediately open mine. I place my hand loosely on the salvo lever, waiting for the lead bombardier to drop his load. At last I see them floating away. I grasp the lever, pull it. It won't budge! I yank harder, but the bombs won't go.

"Bombardier to pilot. The damn bombs won't salvo!"

Johnston activates his control. The plane lurches upward as our 3-ton load drops all at once. I'm so disgusted that I don't even notice where my bombs drop, but I know that they must have fallen off the target.

We continue flying northwest then veer out over the Atlantic, but I hardly care where we're flying. I feel myself edging into a shadowy depression full of self-doubt, self-accusation and self-pity. At least we don't have to bring our bombs back this time, but that's in spite of me. What kind of a bombardier am I? Why should I have had such hard luck? Why can't I get the bombs away? I had always been confident of my skills, but now I begin to question myself, lose my confidence. I'm sure that my second failure will get me in trouble. They might even ground me! The 8th Air Force can't risk crews with a bombardier who can't do his job. I can only hope there had been a serious flaw in the mechanism.

After crossing over the Brest Peninsula, we descend steeply over the channel. By the time we reach Portland Bill, we fly at only 2500 feet, maintaining the low altitude all the way to our base.

Our wheels squeal on the runway at about noontime, seven and one-half hours after take-off, a longer mission than yesterday's. Although heavy with fatigue and disappointment about not having dropped my bombs, I'm greatly relieved that at least some missions can occur without the withering antiaircraft fire that we had endured the day before.

At debriefing I take my shot of bourbon, slipping it to Podoske after he quickly downs his own, swallowing all of it nearly at once like an outlaw at a bar in a Western movie. Again none of the crew reproaches me for my failure, assuming that another malfunction had occurred.

Back in the barracks, I'm too weary to write home, electing instead to take a nap. I hadn't written for several days, unusual for me, but our flying had not only wiped out my time, it had drained my energy. I'd also become so involved in the missions that they'd erased all thoughts of home, our little house on Brett Street and my family seeming very distant.

During the afternoon I learn that there'd been no malfunction of the lever. In order for it to release the bombs, I was supposed to have turned a safety sleeve. I'd never been checked out on one of its type, and no one had bothered to talk to me about its operation. Still, I blame myself for not having known or at least for not asking someone about it. I stew silently in my own gloom. I know that the officers in charge will launch an inquiry.

Later, Intelligence reports that the raid had been a success. Although the Panzer Division had left hours before our arrival, we had destroyed 4 trains stopped in the yard and 2 that were moving. We had also badly damaged the roundhouse. I have no idea what my tardy bombs might have blown up, and I don't want to think about it. That I might have destroyed French homes or killed innocent people begins to haunt me.

THE INTERVIEW

The following morning, after a full night of uninterrupted sleep, I sit on the edge of my bed dashing off a letter to my parents. I hadn't written them in three days. I write that I'd better drop them a line now while I have a chance because we're kept so busy, that except for the sniffles, I'm in good health, but very tired. I let them know I've seen action.

Just after sealing the envelope, I look up to see an officer I don't know entering the barracks. He walks down the aisle between the beds.

"Lieutenant Stevens?" he asks, glancing at each of us.

"I'm Stevens," I reply.

"Captain Smith would like to see you in his office in about fifteen minutes."

"Okay. I'll be there," I tell him as a flutter runs through my body, bees buzzing in my belly.

I'd expected to be called in. After failing to drop my bombs on my first two missions, I knew that I would have to answer for it. This would be it.

I stroll to headquarters, mulling over the answers to probable questions, already letting my emotions run amok. I mutter defensive comebacks under my breath, proclaiming my innocence to myself, then slip back into the shadows of self-doubt. I feel that I'm a victim of bad luck, of unusual circumstances that have cruelly played against me.

The ungodly roar of hundreds of assembling bombers fills the air as I walk; an armada is about to leave for the continent for a late mission. The countryside trembles under their thunderous rumbling. I can feel the vibration of them deep in my body. They're an oscillating swarm, almost terrifying to hear. I can imagine how frightening the sound itself must be to the German people.

For the past two days I'd been part of that sound, a tiny vibration among the many, but after my imminent interview, I might not be. They could ground me. The psychological consequences of such a calamity are too severe for me to even imagine. I'd be crushed. I'd always consider myself a failure, never able to face my parents and friends.

I sit in Captain Smith's office as he slouches behind his messy desk.

"How come, Stevens? You've been on your first two missions, and you haven't dropped your bombs yet."

Uncomfortable in his small office, I try to answer his question.

"On the first raid my bombs simply wouldn't release. I don't know whether it was ice or an electrical malfunction, but they just wouldn't go."

He peers at me from beneath his beat-up hat, its grommet removed to make him look like a hotshot pilot.

"We checked your plane after you landed. The maintenance men found absolutely nothing wrong with the bomb controls. They worked perfectly."

On the defensive now, I screw up my courage.

"I've been bombing from B-17s for a long time, and I know what to do. The system just didn't work at that time. That's all I know."

He hesitates for a moment.

"They say you didn't open the bomb bay doors all the way. If they weren't, the bombs wouldn't have released."

Irritated, I glare at him.

"They were open all the way. The radio man screamed at me that they were open."

"Did the indicator light come on—that they were open?"

"Yes, it was on."

I blurt out my answer without thinking, but at the same time I question myself. Was it on or not? Suddenly I can't remember. I knew it should be on—the red light—but was it?

I hate being put into this miserable position, especially by the man who grills me. I don't like his black moustache and his pale face, his accusing eyes. He looks sick to me. His skin is pallid and unhealthy-looking. The story in the barracks is that he is suffering severe mental stress from his missions, "flak happy." He'd been grounded and given a minor job on the base staff until he recuperated.

I think it unfair for this man to embarrass me, to interrogate me or give me any advice, this man who purports to be in charge, who acts as though he's just climbed out of a cockpit after a daring raid, this pencil-pushing ground jockey with his crumpled war veteran hat.

"What about that second mission? You were supposed to salvo your bombs, but the pilot had to do it for you from the cockpit."

"I'd never had to salvo before, and I had never been checked out on the B-17s lever."

It'd been a simple one with a ball handle. I hadn't known that I had to turn a metal safety sleeve on it to operate it.

"You had bombardier training didn't you, and you'd dropped bombs from a B-17 before, hadn't you? Why didn't you know how to throw the damn thing?"

I have no answer, except that no one had showed me how to use it on this particular B-17, this old clunker with its faulty mechanisms.

"I just hadn't been checked out."

The captain appears to enjoy what he's doing. He becomes animated and aggressive like a weakling who has found a vulnerable quarry who is temporarily weaker, a wounded animal.

He begins to draw away from the specifics into the esoteric, into a higher moral plane.

"You know, Stevens, if you can't do the job, we'll have to ground you. We can't have you endangering the lives of your crew on a useless mission. Your only purpose is to drop bombs on the target. That's the only reason we send the planes out there. We'll give you another chance, but you'll have to come through."

I walk back to the barracks in a whirlwind of dejection and anger. I feel victimized by bad luck. I know that I'm a good bombardier, and I know that I wasn't rattled during those bomb runs. My crew has faith in me. None of them accuses me of bungling.

I struggle too with the possibility that the bomb bay doors might've been just a millimeter away from being all the way open. I can't remember about the damn indicator light. My God! What if I'd put us through all that flak for nothing—that I'd endangered all of our lives for nothing! What if we'd been shot down past the target with our useless bombs still hanging in their racks? The whole mission would have been for naught, and I'd have been responsible. I'd also made Johnston land with three tons of bombs.

I strive to put it all behind me, to regain confidence in myself for the missions ahead, but the familiar clouds of my own depression darken my spirit.

A SUNDAY MORNING

It's Sunday. I'd hoped to attend church service on the base this morning. From the day that combat loomed ahead of me, even back in Louisiana, I'd felt a nameless kind of physical and spiritual nakedness, a vulnerability from which there seemed no refuge. I'd supposed that only God was capable of shielding me. The church, the pastor, the passages from the Bible, the singing of the familiar hymns, all of which I'd known at home, are a powerful attraction to me now, as though a holy protection resides in their music and words.

Instead, we fly in formation at 8,000 feet, having left the English coast over Lincolnshire. We climb steadily over the North Sea on our way to Hamburg to attack the oil refineries in the dock area. We've been warned to expect stiff opposition, but for now we fly a safe route far away from the land. We have two more hours ahead of us before we penetrate the German coast, plenty of time to imagine what the flak will be like over the target. In the bomb bays we carry eighteen 250-pound bombs. The bulge in my pocket is the tagged pins that I'd removed from them.

I carefully go over my procedures. I check the intervalometer and vow to make sure that the bomb bay doors are fully open when it is time to use them. If any problem should develop, it'll not be my fault. I must succeed this time.

Our engines drone monotonously as we continue to climb. The blue sea, with patches of clouds over its face, stretches out before us, a peaceful, relaxing scene that for a while takes my mind off what we are about to do. We fly with our wings tucked in close to each other, the sun glinting off the bare aluminum, the "J" within a black triangle and the red diagonal stripe painted on our rudders. Other groups fly far ahead of us, and many follow us in successive waves. We are part of a maximum effort to destroy Germany's oil production and storage. Today our position is the tail end of the low box, not a good place to be when the flak begins.

By 0900 hours we cross the coast of Germany at 26,000 feet, then fly a feint toward Kiel, with its vast naval facilities, to keep the German trackers busy trying to decide where we're going. Short of Kiel we turn to the south toward Hamburg. I pack my flak suits around me and duck into my helmet.

As we approach Hamburg, I look ahead at the anti-aircraft barrage greeting the first groups over the target. The Germans fill the sky with flak, saturating the area where we must fly straight and level on our bomb runs. Knowing we must plow through it makes my stomach queasy, my guts stir. My life slips into a vacuous limbo, a kind of psychological cocoon where all thoughts are pushed to the edges of consciousness. At the moment, getting through the boiling cauldron ahead seems impossible. I already mutter my prayers, taking sanctuary in the only protection that I know.

The radiomen on all of the planes throw out chaff, masses of what look like stiff Christmas tree icicles, hoping that German radar will bounce off of them, sending false blips on their radar screens to confuse the gunners. The strips twinkle against the deep blue of the high altitude sky, but as yet seem to have little effect.

The bomb bay doors on the lead plane open. I promptly open mine. Among the scattered flak bursts are four coordinated ones that erupt a distance ahead of us, but at exactly our altitude. The next four explode closer, still at our level, the following four closer yet. A battery of German gunners is accurately tracking us. The next volley rears up directly in front of us, the flashes and the black smoke roiling and seething. I know that the next will straddle us.

Antiaircraft fire that had up until now bloomed silently, thuds around us, especially directly beneath our belly, the plane jolting slightly with the concussion. One fragment punches a hole about the size of a silver dollar in my Plexiglas "bay window." Something zips just over my glove. The lead plane's bombs fall away as though in slow motion. I release mine, feeling a small jolt as each one frees itself from the racks. The last bomb floats away, and I close the doors.

Out of the flak now, all four engines miraculously churn, none as yet showing any sign of damage. Beneath and behind us, a huge black column of smoke rises from the dock area. I hope it's from our objective, the Deutche Petroleum works and the Olwerke Julius Schindler.

"Radioman to pilot" says Witherspoon over the intercom, "Caruso's been hit down in the ball turret."

"Well, get him out of there, and see if there's anything you can do for him."

Surely our fuel tanks had been punctured, but so far the self-sealing lining holds up against any major leaks.

Witherspoon's excited voice again crackles over the intercom. "We got Caruso out of the turret, but he's bleeding pretty bad. I've fastened belt tourniquets around the worst places, and dusted sulfa powder in his wounds. He's in bad shape, but I think he'll be okay."

"Roger. Just try to make him as comfortable as possible."

We bank to the right, eventually heading northeast, finally crossing the coast into the relative safety of the North Sea again. Many of our other planes must have had been hit, but none of our group seems to be lost.

"I gave Caruso a morphine syrette to ease his pain. He's about as comfortable as we can make him."

"Roger."

As we head back to England over the sanctuary of the open ocean, I have long stretches of time to run the events of the raid through my mind. The four bursts of flak coming closer and closer and finally enveloping us repeat themselves again and again in my mind. I feel that I had smelled death over Hamburg, had seen it creeping up on us from the front like a grinning black cat, missing us by only a few inches with a deadly swipe of its paw. We'd been only a whisker away from taking a direct hit, from careening crazily down into the German haze. Strangely, I also feel as though I'd beaten death—had faced it at that point, taken its thrust, and come away unscathed. I feel the triumph of it in my soul where it notches up my courage a cosmic millimeter. Or maybe God had protected me as I'd asked. But why didn't He look after Caruso?

We've let down to 13,000 feet by the time we cross the English coast just above Norwich near noontime. We peel off at Polebrook, but fly low near the control tower, shooting a red flare with our Very pistol to let them know that we have a wounded man on board.

After about 5 or 10 minutes Johnston's voice comes over the intercom.

"Pilot to crew. The tower tells me that we have a disabled right wheel. They don't want us to belly land. Too much danger of a fire. We're going to try a regular landing, but I'll try to keep the weight off the wheel as long as possible. I'll keep the right engines going for a little more lift on that side. It could be a rough landing, so secure your selves. An ambulance will meet us after we've landed."

We circle into the landing pattern, Johnston surely concerned about how he's going to handle the plane, how he can prevent a flaming wreck. Our survival is completely dependent on his skill and coolness as a pilot. I move out of the bombardier's seat in the nose, back into the navigator's section. We begin our gradual descent, get into position for our approach.

We settle into the runway as Johnston tries to keep the plane straight. If he doesn't handle it right we'll cartwheel down the runway, and probably break up. Finally, with the plane slowed down as much as possible, Johnston can hold it no longer. We veer to the right off the runway, banging and rattling and bumping out onto the grass where the plane wheels and whips around then comes to an abrupt stop, sending the careening navigator's gun into the small of my back. One wing tilts upward and the other down, but there is no smoke or fire. Johnston had done a masterful job of getting the plane down, and we probably owe our lives to him. Out of the plane, we look up at it, aghast at how much of the sky shows through all of our flak holes.

The emergency crew arrives almost immediately, gently transferring Caruso in his bloody flying suit to a stretcher and then to the waiting ambulance. He's badly hurt, having taken the brunt of the antiaircraft burst just beneath us. Our plane, immobilized, wings askew at the edge of the runway, looks pathetic. A crew will have to come out in a truck to pick us up.

I feel sad about Caruso. He'd always been so talkative and full of life. I liked listening to his Brooklyn accent, but now he's quiet. I still reel from the visions of the hellish flak over Hamburg and the shock of our rough landing, but, strangely, I think about how I'd gotten my bombs away perfectly, again restoring faith in myself.

Eleven other planes from our field had also sustained severe battle damage, and two other men had been wounded, but all of us had somehow returned safely.

The battle damage reported by the mechanics for our plane, #42-97216 of the 509th Squadron is: "Numerous flak holes through left elevator and stabilizer. One hole through tail gunner's compartment. Numerous flak holes both wings, ailerons, ball turret, bottom of fuselage, left and right side of the fuselage, damaging skin, Tokio tanks, feeder tank, tail gunner's window."

They had forgotten to mention our crippled wheel or the hole in the bombardier's window. I begin to doubt whether we can survive the 27 missions that still lie ahead of us.

SELF-CENSORSHIP

Sitting on my bed near the coal stove, I dash off a hasty letter home to my parents. The strains of "I'll Walk Alone" drift through the barracks from a small radio at the other end. Men who have wives or girlfriends at home appear especially touched by the song, but I love it too. Home seems so far away.

Finishing the letter, I stuff it into an envelope and seal it. After addressing it, I must write somewhere on the front, "Censored, Charles N. Stevens, 2nd Lt. A.C." We had been told that we mustn't divulge any details about our missions, including targets, casualties, successes, enemy action or anything at all related to them. We also must not write anything about the base or its operations except for the most mundane activities—going to the movies, the food at the mess hall or whether our mail is coming through. I can't tell anyone where our base is, nor mention any details about the weather.

The men are on their honor not to reveal any vital information that might conceivably be used to advantage by the enemy. Being a good follower of rules, and also fearing that some official might open my mail as a test, I religiously abridge it.

As a result, my letters, all of which had always been full of details, become rather empty. They're as exciting as a sink full of dishwater. My letters become repetitious—"Your mail is not coming through" or "I received four letters from you today." "I am busy" or "tired" or "suffer with the sniffles." "I went to church today" or "a cute cat sleeps in the officers lounge."

Always fascinated by weather, I miss writing details to my father about what to me is an ever-changing drama. England's weather today is Germany's tomorrow or the next day, and I must not give information to the enemy. I'm sure that Germany has spies all over England who regularly report the weather, but they'll get nothing out of me.

I long to tell my parents and friends about how it is to fly in formation with hundreds of other planes, to wrestle with fear or to explain how relieved I feel when we head back across the channel to England. I want to write about what it's like to look down on Germany or France from the brilliant blue of the high-altitude sky or what a shock it is to be awakened for a raid in the darkness of early morning.

Each day I mentally store my experiences, looking forward to the time when I can spill them out. I sometimes imagine myself sitting on the living room couch at home, telling my parents and friends about the extraordinary sights I'd seen and the new feelings that had coursed through me.

I'm sure that some officers write home about their missions anyway, but I, always wanting to do the right thing, comply.

Even if I could write all that I wanted, I wouldn't write about the risks. I wouldn't want to worry them, but I would have liked to unburden myself about feelings that had never touched my life before. On the raid to Hamburg, I had teetered for an instant between existence and non-existence, between being a part of the earth and the universe or not being a part. Never in my young life had I stood at that cosmic threshold before. I think about it, but I can't write a single word.

Instead, even the day after those harrowing experiences, when I'm still full of wild visions and sounds and feelings, I write to my parents only about mundane matters and try to answer their questions—

"Well, I will attempt to write another letter. Your letters seem to get to me in bunches. I didn't receive any for a long time then all of a sudden I got six of them. How are you getting my letters?

"You spoke of seeing Bob Bawolsky at the drug store. I thought he was working in a bank the last time I saw him. He and I were on different teams together. He was in baseball and I in track.

"That's okay what you did with my money.

"You asked about how much money I had. I have plenty. I will be able to send home almost all of every paycheck. I think I spent only 50 cents this week. Indeed, I have spent very little since I left the states.

"I do know the answers to some of your questions, but I can't answer them. We sure will have a lot to talk over when I get home.

"Well, I must get my sleep. I really need it."

I continue to censor my letters. I'm an expert at not letting myself do what most people do, regularly limiting my own actions. It has nothing to do with feeling superior or being self-righteousness; it's just the way I am. I refuse the shot glass of bourbon offered to us after each raid. I reject the offer of a cigarette while everyone else lights up in smoky camaraderie. When that pretty elevator girl in the

Texas hotel had stopped it between floors when I was the only one in it, had looked straight into my eyes, smiled and opened her arms wide to me, I denied her without hesitation. Bewildered, she had turned, and started the elevator again. I had foregone cold beer with the guys at the Officers Club and rolls of the dice as I watched the others in detached amusement. I had had much practice in self-censorship.

I carry my dull letter down the aisle between the beds, holding the red, white and blue-bordered envelope in my fingers. Scribbled in the left hand lower corner, at a slant, are the words, "Censored, Charles N. Stevens, 2nd Lt. A.C."

TWO AFTERNOONS

Heading for France in the late afternoon seems eerie. At least we hadn't had to roll out of our beds in the middle of the night. The angle of the sun causes the sensation, its light now at our backs rather than directly in our eyes. There's something about the quality of the slanting rays that disturbs my biological sense of time, my bodily rhythm, creating the strangeness.

I'd noticed the same effect two days before during our first afternoon raid, a short one to Watten Wood in France. I'd also been heartened that missions, at least the short ones just across the English Channel, were not so dangerous. Finding the primary target obscured by clouds, we'd bombed an airfield at Ypres, Belgium instead, but we had been fired upon only briefly and ineffectually, the widely scattered bursts harmlessly exploding far from any of our planes. The mission had renewed my faith that it might be possible to finish our assigned number. After our close encounter over Hamburg, I'd begun to doubt that we could survive thirty of them.

Just east of Portsmouth our course bends to the left towards the French coast just west of Le Havre. Our target is an oil depot near the Chantiers de Normandie shipyard at Rouen, a large city tucked into one of the varicose-like folds of the Seine. After we've climbed to 25,000 feet over the channel, I begin to prepare myself for what might lie ahead—testing my guns, connecting my chest chute to my harness, and like a medieval knight, donning my armor of flak jackets. I sit in my bombardier's seat, peering out from beneath my oversized helmet at France and the lumpy blanket of clouds extending from the coast inland. We pass over the beaches, gradually turning to our left once, then again toward Rouen.

As we approach the target, the leaden smear of anti-aircraft fire up ahead indicates that this raid will not be like the "milk run" of the previous afternoon. The Germans are vigorously protecting their dwindling oil reserves. Although the flak barrage is not as intense as that at Hamburg, the gunners appear to be well trained and accurate with their fire. Knowing we must fly through it on the bomb run gives rise to that same queasy numbness I had felt before. We're to be ducks in a German shooting gallery. I lean away slightly, and silently mutter the only prayer I know, but I'm ready to drop the bombs.

Over the target with our bomb bays open, we begin to taste their marksmanship, their antiaircraft shells blossoming among us like black flowers in a cruel garden. They dog us with their tracking, sniffing and nipping at our heels. The plane just off our right wing begins to smoke and drop back, then slowly falls in a lazy spiral. Five parachutes open, floating earthward like feathered dandelion down, before the plane explodes into a ball of persimmon-colored fire. Although consumed with the preservation of my own skin, I mourn for them, a few quiet words falling from my lips. Some of the beds in our barracks would lie empty tonight.

Soon after closing the bomb bay doors, the flak suddenly ceases, the gunners probably choosing to concentrate their fire on the new groups coming in behind us. In spite of the barrage, I'd gotten my bombs away smoothly. We pass out into the clear, cold purity of the high atmosphere, all four engines still running smoothly. We bank to the left, taking the shortest route to the French coast and the relative safety of the English Channel. We touch down at the base just before 8:30 pm with still plenty of light left in the long summer day.

* * *

"Sixty-four fuckin' holes!" shouts Lieutenant Ziwicki as he bursts through our barracks door, his head cocked slightly upward, his eyes as wide as political campaign buttons.

He strides through the barracks between the rows of beds, repeating him self.

"Sixty-four fuckin' holes!"

"Yeah. The crew chief counted 'em. Sixty-four fuckin' holes! God damn that flak was accurate!"

All of us had taken our share of German steel, and we'd lost one plane. Our crew chief had pried a jagged fragment of flak about the size of a large marble from our wing shortly after we had wheeled into our hardstand, and had given it to me as a souvenir. I hold the sharp-edged metal lump in the palm of my hand, moving it around with the tip of my finger, the fragment's cold hardness contrasting with the softness of my hand. I gently press the jagged missile into my skin.

Having proclaimed his battle damage, Ziwicki, afloat in the turbulence of his emotions, wrestling with his terror, leaves to spread his news to other barracks.

"Sixty-four fuckin' holes," he mutters as he disappears through the back door.

TOULOUSE

The triangular shape of Selsey Bill, a landform jutting out into the English Channel like an arrowhead pointing at France, is becoming quite familiar. We'd used the landmark just east of Portsmouth as a leaving place and a return spot on several missions. We fly over it now at 17,000 feet, headed south for a mission deep into southern France at Toulouse, a city only 75 miles from the jagged peaks of the Pyrenees and the Spanish border. In order to reach our target, a military airfield, we have to fly hundreds of miles over enemy-held France, a situation that none of us relish. We climb slowly now, our engines throbbing and straining to lift the weight of full fuel tanks and a heavy bomb load to an altitude of 25,000 feet, finally attaining it just before crossing into France midway between Le Havre and Cherbourg.

Our mission is already behind schedule. We had had to assemble near our field at 17,000 feet instead of the planned 11,000 feet due to thick layers of clouds. We took off at 0430, again after being rousted out of a sound sleep. Already weary, we've a ten-hour flight ahead of us before we can stretch out on our beds again.

We'd flown out and in over Selsey Bill yesterday and the day before on "Noball" missions to coastal France where we had hoped to bomb launching sites for V-1 buzz bombs, the rocket motor-propelled missiles that had been plaguing London, the first of Hitler's revenge weapons. The first mission was near Abbeville where we dropped our 250-pound bombs by radar through a solid undercast. Because of the cloud cover we couldn't see the results of our bombing. For a change, the flak had been meager and wild. The second was a raid on a launching site near Crepy. Flak had been light but accurate on the bomb run, slightly damaging six of our planes. We ran into uncharted flak just as we were leaving the French coast, possibly from mobile units that had been moved in.

By now we'd completed seven missions. This one is our eighth. I try to take them one at a time, and not dwell on the twenty-three or possibly twenty-eight we have left before they'll send us home.

We have hours before we reach the target. My mind wanders. I look closely at the land below, deciding that, at least from the vantage point of five miles up, the French countryside looks better and the houses more beautiful than those of England. Vast green fields and dark forests spread out below us. Roads converge into villages, the buildings appearing scrubbed, gleaming in the sunlight. Above all it seems peaceful, as though the country is not at war. I think about the illusion of viewing the land from such a lofty height where people and machines are largely invisible. Perhaps I project a kind of tranquility on the land because I want the war to be over. I allow myself to dream of traveling in all that beauty some day.

We alter our course slightly as some of the groups ahead of us run into anti-aircraft fire. By changing our heading by only a few degrees we're able to avoid it. Squadrons of P-47 fighters accompany us part of the way, discouraging any attacks by the Luftwaffe. Just seeing the blunt-nosed Thunderbolts in formation, the sun glinting off their polished aluminum, gives us confidence.

Finally, shortly before 10 am we approach the airfield at Toulouse. Smoke bombs dropped by the lead groups trace puffy arcs from the planes down to the field, the several smoke streams appearing like the unsteady legs of a gigantic spider. Shifting currents at different altitudes soon begin to tear them apart, turning the legs into crooked appendages. I open the bomb bay doors, and look toward the lead plane. The usual greeting begins to burst around us, but the Germans, in spite of their accuracy, apparently have only a few batteries to guard the airport. The lead plane's bombs fall away silently, and I release mine.

A smoke screen obscures much of the airfield. Some of our bombs blast an open area south of the hangers and runways; others rip up the ground a mile short of the target. After hours of tedious flying to reach the airfield, little had been accomplished.

Immediately after releasing our bombs, we turn toward the northwest and a quick path to the sea, leaving the French coast near Bordeaux. Now over the Atlantic we begin the long trip home, making a series of doglegs over the water to take the shortest route to England without passing over the Brest Peninsula. I feel safer now. I had weathered another encounter, this one long and tiring, but with little enemy opposition. I am buoyant and optimistic. I have my life and my limbs, and the resolve to take on the next mission. I feel that everything will be all right, that I will complete my tour of duty in regular order, and go home.

We make landfall over the tip of Cornwall, at Lizard Point near Land's End. All the planes are low on fuel after the long flight, several of them having to land at British airports in southern England for refueling. Our plane has just enough gas to return to Polebrook where we land at 1430, 10 hours after taking off.

My body aches with fatigue. The long flight, the tension and the hours on oxygen had taken their toll. We had flown missions four days in a row now, and I yearn for a respite. After a late lunch in the mess hall, I lie down on my bed, letting my body sink deliciously into it. Last Sunday I had wanted to go to church but had flown to Hamburg instead. Here it is Sunday again, and I have missed church once more by flying the interminable mission to Toulouse. I soon drop off to sleep.

A BICYCLE RIDE IN THE COUNTRY

Fighting our way back through the English weather had been the most difficult part of the mission to Laon Couvron where we had successfully bombed an airfield. We took off at five in the morning, had flown east across the English Channel to the Dutch islands then abruptly south to the target in northern France.

We descended steeply over the English Channel on our way home, dropping from 25,000 feet over the Dutch islands to only 4000 feet when we roared in over the British coast. A solid mass of clouds lay beneath us, a barrier to the standard landing patterns of our formations. Alternate airports were assigned. Finally, like a rip in a blanket, a small hole opened up in the cloud deck, allowing one element of the formation at a time to slip through. The weather improved as we neared our airfield at Polebrook, the afternoon sky opening up to a glorious blue with powder puff clouds.

Weary and still tense from our long mission, Podoske and I decide to get on our bicycles, find a country road and ride it as far as we can.

Outside the guarded entrance to the air base, we point our bicycles down the first small road we see, one that appears only wide enough for a single car. Pedaling down the narrow road that winds through the low green hills, I feel buoyantly free, my soul releasing like a party balloon. We dash by the fields and pass in and out cloud shadows.

We feast on the green hills, the trees rocking gently in the afternoon wind, the grass and wild flowers trembling at the side of the road. We inhale the purity of the country air, and feel the gentle warmth of the sun on our faces. I'm a tight bud opening up after the constriction of our missions—the darkness, the cramped quarters, the cumbersome weight of flak vests and the binding discomfort of oxygen masks. I am a hedgehog unrolling from the clinched coiling of our emotions, the tightness that creeps along my neck, taut wires pulling at my shoulders and back.

We lift our faces to the sun like sunflowers as we churn with our legs. The stretched guitar strings in my body go slack. I listen to the wind whistling past my ears, inhale the fragrances of wild grasses and grain fields.

The sun ducks behind swelling clouds, the nearest one now as dark as bruises on its underside. The first drops of rain splatter against our faces. With a sudden deluge imminent, we look around for the nearest shelter. Just over a rise is a hayshed close to the road. We turn into the dirt path leading to the farm, the owner's dog barking at our intrusion. Bumping over ruts, we roll under the metal roof, parking our bicycles next to the haystacks. The intoxicating smell of the hay reminds me of the farm in California where my sister and I spent such a wonderful summer staying with relatives. That was only three short years ago, when we were still in high school.

Raindrops patter and ping on the tin above us, but the heavier portion of the shower only grazes us.

As we wait for the rain to stop, a small boy about 8 or 9 years old hustles out of the farmhouse to where we lean against the hay bales. A friendly boy with tousled hair, a sprinkling of freckles across his face and a broad smile, he is very excited about finding two Yank airmen in uniform on his own farm.

"Hello," he says shyly.

"Hi there," we reply. "We were out riding our bicycles and turned in here to get out of the rain."

He looks at us curiously and asks, "Did you do your job today?"

"Yes we did, this morning."

"What kind of plane do you fly?"

"We fly large planes. Bombers. Our airfield is not far from here."

"Oh."

For some reason I am amazed and amused that a child of his age speaks with such a distinct British accent, as if I thought he would have to grow into it. As we talk with him I realize how pleasant it is to be around a child again. After having only associated with airmen and living completely in the Air Force world for so long, I had lost the real world of farmers, the smell of hay and the innocence of children.

"Well, we better go now. We've got to move on. It was nice talking to you. Thanks for the shelter. Good-bye now."

"Good-bye."

With the shower past, we sail out on to the wet road, our tires hissing on the pavement. The rain has brought out all of the earth smells, the pungent scents of damp plants and fields. With the threat of further downpours, we decide to head back to the base.

We return by way of the small village of Oundle where Podoske, thirsty from the exercise of the ride, wants to have a beer. I tell him I'll have a Coca-Cola with him. A lone man nurses a glass of stout at the far end of the pub. Podoske is disappointed that the beer is "warm", not chilled as it is at home or even on the base. He drinks it anyway, mildly complaining. Again it is nice to be off of the base, even if it is a pub, where "real people" stop by for a pint and a game of darts.

Back at the base, back in the military world, the war world, I am still weary, but psychologically I bask in a freshness I have not known in a while. I should sleep well tonight.

THE LETTER

Sitting on the edge of his bunk, Lieutenant Wallace reads one of his letters from home. Suddenly he whacks the back of his hand against the paper as though slapping someone across the cheek. The sharp snap of it startles me.

"Oh Christ! She's been to Los Angeles. Oh my God!"

A frown creases his forehead. He peers angrily across the room, his eyes shooting sparks like steel on an emery wheel.

"I know why she went there! I know why!"

He vents his temper, not caring who hears him. He springs to his feet, paces the barracks floor, the letter crumpled in his large hand. Only a half dozen men are about, all of us watching him with a kind of awestruck fascination.

"If my wife's going into L.A., she can't be up to any good. Damn it! I know why she's going there!"

He raves as he prances around, the late afternoon light slanting in through the doorway.

"Here I am, stuck on this damned island, and I can't do anything about it! Damn her!"

He briefly lights on his bed once more, muttering to himself, jams the letter in his pocket. Leaping up again, he stalks out of the barracks. "I know what she went there for," he mumbles as he bursts out the door.

I sit on my bunk, writing a letter to my parents. After Wallace had begun to shout, I looked up at him, amazed by his tirade, his obvious pain. I can only guess why he's so disturbed. Apparently he doesn't trust his wife. I suppose that when she goes into Los Angeles, she meets other men, that he feels betrayed. It seems to me that he must have suffered the same problem before, or he wouldn't be so sure about her motives.

It's remarkable to me how a letter from home can devastate him so, this tall athletic specimen who's built like a fullback, this handsome guy with his dark red hair and classic manly features, this strutting cocksure pilot. The letter has brought him down psychologically just as surely as a German fighter plane might have shot him down physically.

Soon after dusk all of us slip into our beds and turn off the lights, anticipating the possibility of an early wake-up call for a mission. Wallace has still not returned. The rhythmic sounds of breathing begin to blend with the darkness. I lie in the silence, thinking about home—the wind in the casuarina trees, my dog Pal, the voices of my parents, the sounds of the house where it was always safe.

Just before I drift off to sleep, Wallace bolts through the back door, staggers through the dark and lunges into the unlit coal stove, sending the vent pipes rolling and clanging across the floor.

"God damn it!" he slurs in his alcoholic voice. "Jesus Christ!"

As the stove is near my bed, the impact of the rattling pipes and his heavy unsure steps shock me out of my reverie.

"Hey! Knock it off there," yells Johnston. "We're trying to get some sleep."

"Shut up Johnston. I'll yell if I want to. So, just shut up!"

Johnston, considering that Wallace is big, drunk and angry, wisely says no more. We don't know what the soused pilot will do next. He sways next to my bed, but then stumbles on to find his own in the dark. He struggles out of his uniform, breathing heavily, and muttering words we can't understand. I do hear him say, "I know why she went there". With the help of the liquor he had apparently been drinking all evening at the Officers' Club, he soon drops off to a restless sleep.

Against the enemy we do what we must, worrying more about our own safety than anything else. Secondarily, we deal with each other, form friendships and bind into a kind of togetherness, a loose camaraderie. But our authentic selves, who we are, our real lives, are tied to those we love thousands of miles away, all of them connected tenuously to us by a steady flow of letters from home. Words of concern and love cheer us up, raise our morale, soften our loneliness, but the sharp edges of disturbing words can cut into us deeply.

THE AIR MEDAL

Spiffed up in our dress uniforms, we stand at attention on the concrete ramp near the great repair hangars. Several planes awaiting patching up cast their shadows on the oil-dappled concrete near us. The colonel addresses us, but his words are far away, dispersed by the gentle breeze so that we hear only fragments.

"Gentlemen, it is an honor for me to present you with these Air Medals. The Air Medal is a tribute to your courage and skill…It is through your extraordinary achievements…we'll win this war…The Army Air Force is proud of you all."

Finally the colonel, peering from beneath the shadow of his cap, presents us with the medals, one by one. To each man he mutters, "Congratulations."

After the ceremony, I walk away, boyishly proud of my Air Medal. I'd really done nothing special or outstanding to earn it. The automatic awarding of the Air Medal means that I've survived seven missions. I'd been able to hoist myself into the bomber, endure the flak, drop my bombs and return unharmed. I'd been able to fly over Paris, Angouleme, Hamburg, Watten, Rouen and two buzz bomb launching sites on the coast of France without being shot down or severely injured. I—God, Fate, Fortune or Luck—do deserve some kind of medal, some token of appreciation, I suppose.

Back in the barracks we open the flat oblong boxes. The bronze metal clicks against the sides. So there it is, a medal. If we survive seven more missions, we can add an oak leaf cluster to our ribbons—and for every seven after that.

"Makes you feel like a veteran, doesn't it?" says Warren, our navigator.

"Yeah, but we're just starting. We still have 23 damn missions to go. A lot can happen. We're a long ways from going home. Maybe the medals won't mean a thing."

"Well, at least it's a start, one small step along the way."

We put them away without further comment. They would be something to take home, but we can't think about that yet.

* * *

Not long after I had received the medal, my parents send me a clipping that had appeared in our Inglewood paper. A small headline reads: "Lt. Charles Stevens Decorated With Air Medal for Achievement". Following the headline is: "AN EIGHTH AAF BOMBER STATION, England—Second Lt. Charles N. Stevens, 535 Brett St., Inglewood, B-17 Flying Fortress bombardier, has been decorated with the Air Medal for 'meritorious achievement' on bombing attacks on enemy Europe. The citation accompanying the award read in part, 'The courage, coolness and skill displayed by this officer upon these occasions reflect great credit upon himself and the Armed Forces of the United States.'

Lt. Stevens, 19 years old, son of Mr. and Mrs. Charles K. Stevens, has taken part in seven combat missions. He was a student at Inglewood High School before entering the service April 8, 1943."

I had rightfully earned a medal for going through the agonizing tension of the missions, but words like "meritorious", "courage", "coolness" and "skill" seem to imply that I'd done something extraordinary like saving someone's life, bringing the plane in single handed, carrying on while wounded or helping others with no regard for my own safety, the feats usually attached to heroes.

I don't feel heroic. I don't think any of us do. We all know what we must do, and we perform our tasks the best we can. We fly with great apprehension and deal with our fears during the long moments of danger. When the enemy attempts to knock us down, we face the danger with stoicism, prayer, anger or whatever individual capacity we have to cope. After seeing with our own eyes what can happen to airplanes, we do have the courage or maybe resignation, possibly a blend of the two, to board our bombers again, and strike out on another mission. To refuse to fly a potentially dangerous raid is unthinkable. For all of this we deserve an award, an appreciation for what we've been through, a medal for our morale to keep us going. I'll be able to wear the blue and orange ribbon next to the European Theater ribbon on my tunic, just below my bombardier's wings.

Press notices had been sent to the hometown papers of all of the men awarded Air Medals that day. They keep the home front satisfied, and make them proud of us and consequently of themselves. In a sense, the press notices serve as their medals too.

A NEED FOR SANCTUARY

Even before I'd flown any missions at all, I'd begun to yearn for church services. Apprehensive about flying in combat, I longed for a sense of safety or protection. I thought about the security of my home and the sanctuary of my own church in Los Angeles. Today I lie on my bunk imagining myself sitting in church on a bright Sunday morning, everyone all dressed up, content. I think about the time after church, the kids all running around on the lawn, innocently screaming and laughing. I'm surprised how much I miss such ordinary events now that they've been taken away from me.

On two consecutive Sundays I'd flown missions to Hamburg and Toulouse, both missions sucking out so much of my vitality that I'd had no strength left for evening service. I miss being able to go to church, the strain of eight missions only increasing my appetite for spiritual solace. I'd only been able to attend church once since we'd been assigned to the base, but I feel a need to go more often.

The following Sunday the sun wakes us up rather than the crusty sergeant with his miserable flashlight. We'd enjoyed three consecutive days of rest, and today's Sabbath will add a fourth. For the first time in three weeks I should be able to make my way to the chapel.

During the past few free days I'd been able to ride my bicycle through the woods to the base movie theater and finally wash out my underwear, which had been "unfit for human use". I now have a whole

79

drawer of fresh clean shorts, undershirts and socks neatly folded, a pleasant sight. Perhaps the neat order of my drawer is symbolic of the restored order in my life after a respite from the disorder of the missions, but, more importantly, I sorely need to reestablish my spiritual life.

I write to my parents: "Finally got a chance to go to church again Sunday. We have a very good chaplain here, and I enjoy him very much. We have a very informal service, but very nice. We sing hymns; have responsive readings and prayers as well as a short, interesting sermon. We have a very small G I organ that the weather officer plays for us. High-ranking officers in full dress uniforms as well as mechanics in their greasy fatigue suits fill the room. That's what I like about it. It's always very populated on Sunday mornings."

I'd never been particularly religious at home. I can never remember actually wanting to go to church services, attending them for the most part, at times reluctantly, simply as a matter of tradition or to please my parents. Sometimes I'd stayed home on Sunday while the rest of the family had gone to church, feeling I'd weaseled out of something, and that I had a lovely few hours of freedom ahead to do what I wanted.

Even after I'd entered the Air Corps I'd only begun to feel the need of the spiritual, especially as I grew homesick after having been away for so long. Somehow, going to church was like being home. As the prospect of being sent overseas and into combat drew closer, I found myself being attracted even more to the church, this time, I suppose, because of a deep need for divine protection.

I need them both now, the safety of home and the mercy of God to shield me from death or injury. I can protect myself from flying shrapnel with flak jackets and a helmet, but I can do nothing to shield the plane. For that I feel the need for divine providence.

But other than praying, I need to strengthen my inner self—to add a degree of courage to my stoic endurance. I listen intently to the words that pass from the chaplain's lips, hoping for a balm, assuring phrases that will soften my feelings of vulnerability. I admire him, but I never hear what I'm hoping for, whatever that is. Once he had said to all of us, "Sometimes I'm at my wit's end, trying to think of what I need to say to you." He'd attempted to be honest with us, but he'd shaken me. I'd depended on him for the word and the way, yet I don't give up hope that I'll hear it.

CHARLES N. STEVENS

THE FOURTH OF JULY

We'd flown over Selsey Bill, the triangular projection of land on the coast near Portsmouth, so many times that I can now recognize it quite easily. When we headed for France or the Low Countries or returned to England, we often used it as a landmark because of its distinctive shape. I can only imagine it this morning as layers of clouds smother it and the channel. We fly over it at 21,000 feet, still climbing, on our way to Saumur, France, to destroy a bridge. Each of us carries two two-thousand-pound bombs, as big as boilers, enough destructive power to twist the thick girders of bridges into grotesque steel pretzels.

The day doesn't seem like the Fourth of July to me. In our grim business, each day is rather hazy, the days of the week, even holidays, distorted into an unfocused blur of time. Even the hours of the day become meaningless because we have no set routine, sometimes leaving on missions in the afternoon or more often at dawn after rising in the dark at three o'clock in the morning. Some days we don't fly at all.

We steadily gain altitude over the channel so that by the time we arrive at the French coast we'll reach 25,000 feet. This Independence Day is not like the "real" ones, those with flashing firecrackers and fireworks that erupt into glittering fountains of silver fire, with lighted pellets that transform themselves into ashy snakes, with sparklers whirled by children, tracing fiery designs in the night. I remember how the ghostly glow of fireworks lit up the casuarina trees on our street and the pungent clouds of smoke rolled down it with the sea wind. I'd always loved that sulfurous fragrance.

By the time we cross the coast south of Le Havre, our bombers trail long streams of vapor in the moist air. They blend together to form a ragged layer behind each of the formations, cutting down the visibility for the groups that follow. We alter our course slightly to avoid the contrails of the flight in front of us.

Near the target antiaircraft fire begins to burst around our formation, but the German gunners, apparently firing in desperation, launch few shells, most of them erratic. The chance that they'll get lucky, however, is always possible. At the same time that we fly into the swirling contrails of the formation ahead a flak shell explodes near us. Our plane suddenly twists violently up and to the right. I'm sure we've been hit, that we're beginning to roll out of control. The patterns of shadow and sun quickly change in the nose. The Plexiglas frames more of the blue sky above. I snap on the other bracket of my chest parachute, listen for the signal to bail out. I haven't had time to be frightened. I glance back toward the escape hatch, ready to go. I'm locked in an adrenaline suspension.

"Pilot to crew. We're okay. It's just prop wash from the groups ahead. We'll settle down in a minute."

"Roger, bombardier. My God I almost left!"

We buck and jolt, the planes sidling away from each other so they'll not tangle in the tight formation.

Down behind my flak jacket my heart thumps, my shot of adrenaline spent. I now feel the fear and excitement of what I thought to be a crisis, bailing out of our crippled airplane. As my pulse settles down, I sense the relief of not having had to jump. I begin to see a flicker of humor in it all—Stevens ready to bail out because we wallow around in a little prop wash.

Below, all of France seems blanketed with a solid deck of clouds, only a few small holes visible here and there. As we have no radar plane with us today, we must bomb visually, hoping for a break in the undercast.

"Pilot to bombardier."

I respond with two clicks of the intercom.

"The lead plane can't find the target so we're gonna have to make a second pass."

Two clicks.

We fly in a large circle, a 360, so that we can make another run on the elusive bridge. No one likes to spend extra time like this over hostile territory, giving the gunners one more chance at us. I'm angry that we have to go through it again. By the time we settle into our second bomb run, the break in the clouds that the lead bombardier spotted closes up.

With visual bombing impossible, we head for home. I'm uneasy about having to carry the heavy bombs back to the field, landing with them. Even though they probably wouldn't explode, even in a crash, their added weight will necessitate adjustments in landing. One bombardier, either leery of landing with them or their plane low on fuel, dumps his bombs in the channel.

We begin to let down over the water, heading for Beachy Head on the southern coast of England. It'd been a strange Fourth of July with fireworks of another sort, our bombs that had not even gone off. Even the antiaircraft fire had been generally light and inaccurate, a fact that greatly pleased and relieved me. I had flown 10 missions now, one-third of the missions I must complete, and the relative ease of this one had again given me confidence that I might finish the rest of them.

We skirt London around its east side, landing at Polebrook shortly after ten. Although I'm excited about completing another mission, a "milk run" of sorts, I wonder why the mission had been called at all. Why would the bomber command send out planes when they knew that the target would more than likely be obscured by clouds? Why didn't they send a radar plane with us?

I'd been up since three o'clock in the morning. Exhausted from the early call and the tension of the mission, I crawl into the sack to sleep it off. I think briefly about the fun and thrills of all of the Fourth of Julys I had ever known at home, and then I sleep.

NOBALL

We'd flown two Noball missions before. Now we're on our way to another. I don't even know what the word means, only that it has something to do with the German buzz bombs that are creating havoc in London. Simply large bombs with wings and a pulse-rocket engine on top, the V-1s are launched from massive ski jump-like structures near the coasts of France, just across the English Channel. They're causing so much isolated physical damage and general psychological distress in London that their launching sites have become primary targets.

Shortly after nine in the morning we fly over familiar Selsey Bill, this time having already reached our bombing altitude of 25,000 feet, our target less than an hour away. We fly in the high box today, a formation of twelve bombers flying slightly higher than the lead box that is down and in front of us. The low box is behind the lead and slightly lower. Thirty-six bombers make up the group from our field, each of us carrying a dozen 500-pound bombs. Several groups from other fields fly ahead of and behind us.

On our way across the water I briefly think about my parents, my thoughts prompted by the letter I'd received from them yesterday. They had waffles for breakfast, a simple mundane bit of news that stirs my imagination that quickly takes me back home. I'd answered their letter last night—"So you had waffles for breakfast. I never used to be very crazy about them, but I think I would be now." I'd thought about the waffles, the butter melting over them, the amber syrup filling up the little square holes. I thought more about where I would be eating them—in the quiet security of our breakfast nook at home. I remember how the batter oozed out of the sides of the waffle iron like creamy lava, the wisps of steam that rose when my father lifted the lid, the fragrance. I recall the wooden bench seats creaking and snapping ever so slightly when we sat down or got up.

I'd gone on to write—"You know, since I've been in the army, I've learned to eat eggplant. Now I guess I like everything. At least the army hasn't had much trouble pleasing me with chow." I'd thought about the way my mother prepared eggplant, squashed and creamed or smashed then fried in evil-tasting fritters.

My parents had just learned that I was in England. Here I am flying my 11th mission, and they've just discovered where. I blame the slow mail on the Normandy invasion, and the secrecy surrounding it.

My mother writes that they have new orders for flexible metal hoses, parts for aircraft engines that they silver-solder in our garage at home. I see them out there in the bluish fluorescent light with their "engineer's" caps on, smoke rising from the bright arcs of their torches as they affix brass fittings.

Shortly before 1000 hours we arrive at the target, the launching ramp at Bertreville St. Ouen. So far, antiaircraft fire has been meager. The lead box and low box bomb the target, the explosions erupting in dense plumes of brown smoke, pulverized earth and debris.

"Pilot to bombardier."

I double click.

"They tell me that our lead bombardier can't see the target because of all the smoke. We're going to take a wide turn and come back at it again."

"Okay. I don't like it, but I guess we have to."

On the second run we release our bombs, most of them striking bare ground to the right of the ramp. The other boxes from our group had headed straight for England after their runs, leaving us by ourselves. I feel insecure about being abandoned.

Soon after our bomb run, the German gunners at Dieppe begin firing, laying some bursts right in among us. Since there are just 12 planes in our formation, isolated from the rest, they can concentrate their fire. Shortly afterward, two of our planes, badly damaged, leave the formation, apparently heading for the nearest airfield in England.

We let down at the French coast, lowering to 18,000 feet by the time we reach Beachy Head. Beholding the coast of England is always a beautiful experience. Approaching its cliffs and beaches means that we've completed another mission, that we're going to return safely, that we're going to be whole for another day. The euphoria that lifts our spirits after a safe return is the psychological spark that gives us the courage to fly the next mission.

We land at Polebrook shortly before eleven, a good part of the day still left to us. After lunch I nap away the tension of the mission and think about our two-day pass to London beginning tomorrow. Johnston, Warren and I had visited the city of

Peterborough with two other men, but it was not far from our field. We'd been entranced by the lofty silence of its cathedral. We'd also attended a corny vaudeville show. The acts had been amateurish, and the skits hadn't been funny. I write in a letter home afterwards—"British humor must be slightly different from ours."

But London offers much more, and I look forward to visiting all of its wonders. Being off the base and away from bombers and missions and waking up in the middle of the night will be a great relief.

CHARLES N. STEVENS

A TWO-DAY PASS TO LONDON

In a flurry of steam, and a blast from its shrill whistle, the train puffs into Peterborough. I can't get used to the British locomotive whistles, so different from the mellow, deep-toned harmonies of those back home. Driving rods clank as it rolls by, and steam hisses and snorts out of valves and fittings. I miss the cowcatcher and solid coupler in front, the British engines having only two round odd-looking buffers that protrude forward.

Passengers already stand in the aisles and vestibules of the coaches, or carriages as they call them. Johnston, Warren, Podoske and I force our selves on to the train, jostling other passengers to find standing space. I work myself into a place where I can at least look through a partially blocked window. The old cars, grimy and worn, burdened with humanity, finally edge out of the station, the locomotive chugging mightily with its load.

I feel light-hearted, not only because we're going off to a new adventure in London, but also because we're away from the field, and, although many military men ride the train, I'm at least among some civilians again. For two days, anyway, I can forget about bombing missions and the war.

The English countryside fascinates me. Even when we fly, I like looking down at the strange mosaic of fields bordered by hedges, the geometric remnants of forests, the slow rivers winding through the hills. I like peering down at villages and towns connected to each other like ganglia with nerve-like roads and railroads. I gaze out of the train window at the verdant hills and fields as they flash by, some of them dotted with sheep. The soft green soothes and comforts me, rests my eyes, enters my body like a long deep breath, nourishes my mind. Swans glide on some of the glassy rivers in a setting so peaceful that the specter of war seems thousands of miles away, in another era even.

Eventually we leave the countryside behind, replacing it with the dirty tenements and industrial buildings of outer London. We zip over and under bridges, roar through tunnels and past piles of rubble before we glide into Kings Cross Station. Clouds and smoke press down on London, the haze almost as thick as fog. A huge locomotive dulled by the pall backs out of the station, its billows of steam merging with the smoky air. I can just make out the initials, L N E R, London Northeast Railroad, on its long tender.

Outside the station, we join a polite but anxious queue waiting for taxis, a parade of black cabs pouring into the driveway outside. "Mayfair Hotel", we shout as we hustle into ours. We neither know much about the Mayfair, nor where it is, but one of the more experienced crewmembers had recommended it to us, had said it was a nice place to stay. Our cab driver cuts through the London traffic as we brace ourselves, especially when he whips around corners. Three of us sit on the regular seat while Podoske sits on a small pull-down type.

"There's really a lot of space back here. It's like we've got our own little room," says Podoske.

"Yeah, it's stark though. Nothing much to hang on to when we take the corners," replies Johnston.

"I'd rather not look ahead at where we're going. It's better to watch what happens out at the side. This guy likes to live dangerously."

I'm agog at the buildings flying by, strange-looking old stone structures so unlike our own, most of them grimy with coal dust.

At the Mayfair, which appears rather grand to us compared to the spartan atmosphere of our barracks, the desk clerk assigns our rooms, one for Johnston and Warren and another for Podoske and me. The rooms are clean and neat, the beds comfortable. We have our own private bathroom, a luxury.

Soon after settling into our rooms, we're out on the street again, merging with the throngs that crowd the sidewalks, a mixture of soldiers and civilians. Many are British soldiers wearing berets. Interspersed among them are small groups of their officers. I consider them to be pretentious as they strut by clutching their riding crops and gloves in one hand as part of their uniform, even though I doubt if they're ever near horses. Some wear polished brown leather boots as well. I begin to realize that the British are very fond of their traditions, carrying them on far past their usefulness.

We soon discover that it's easy to become lost in London as the streets, instead of being laid out in a grid as most American cities are, follow the ancient roads, perhaps muddy paths that once led through old London to the market places. The angles and curves soon confound our sense of direction, but the Londoners, always polite as though they genuinely like us, interrupt their jaunty walks to help us out, constantly ending their directions with, "You can't miss it." I like their rapid directions and their clipped British accents, even when I don't understand everything they've said.

Although we aren't looking for it, we eventually find ourselves at Picadilly Circus, a part of London that every airman, every soldier in England, knows about, home of the "Picadilly Commandos", London's horde of prostitutes. We walk through at dusk, in the gathering darkness of London's blackout. Some of them sit on the filthy sidewalk, their backs up against the brick buildings, their knees drawn up, their legs spread carelessly. They remind me of the Mexican whores I had seen in Nuevo Laredo and fill me with the same double feelings of revulsion and sympathy. Some carry flashlights then take their potential customers back between the buildings where they shine the light down inside the front of their dresses to show them what they'll be getting. One wraps her arms around Johnston, lets them slide down his body until she nearly tackles him.

"Oh, come on Yank. Let's go. I like you. Let's have some fun!"

Another sidles up to Podoske, an innocent-like sweetness in her voice.

"I'm really good. You'll like me. I know just what to do. Okay Sweetheart?"

None of them approach me. We walk on, keeping our legs moving, our heads to the front as much as possible, as though we plow through a hostile crowd or a pack of menacing dogs.

Back at the Mayfair we have our first meal in their dining room. We don't have much on our plates and really have to pay for it. A meal I could have for 50 cents in the States costs $4. While we eat dinner, the air raid sirens sound again as more buzz bombs are on their way to London. We had heard their mournful sound during the afternoon, a plaintive dirge of whines and moans and overtones, like the wailing of a chorus of wolves. We had seen barrage balloons, like fat silver sausages, hovering over the east side of London to snag the low-flying missiles with their steel cables.

The following day Podoske and I set off to see the sights of London. Down near the Thames we look up at the Neo-Gothic magnificence of the Parliament Building and the ornate tower housing Big Ben, now silenced for the duration. On radio news reports from London we had always heard its deep tones as a symbol of British steadfastness, bravery and "pluck."

We move on to Westminster Abbey, and tilt back our heads to take in its Gothic arches, its pointed pediments reaching toward the clouds. We gaze out on the sluggish Thames with its slow-moving shipping, the river much broader than I thought it would be.

During nights in my bed at home, just before I'd entered the service, I'd thought about London, feeling somehow that I would go there. In the secure comfort of my covers I tried to imagine it at the mercy of the German Blitz, the unrelenting bombing by the Luftwaffe. In my mind I saw fires raging, buildings collapsing in smoke and flame, heroic firemen with their hoses silhouetted against the conflagration. I'm surprised when I actually see the city, that it appears largely intact, at least the small area where Podoske and I have walked. We'd seen parts of blocks leveled to rubble here and there, some recently in encounters with buzz bombs, but nothing compared to the horror that I had imagined, a vision fueled by newsreels and radio descriptions.

We walk past the gray stone of the Tower of London then on to St. James Park. Except for the long line of trenches dug in the park, refuges for Londoners caught in the open during raids, the park lies peaceful and green. A gray-haired couple sit on a park bench, their lips together in a long kiss. Their unending embrace appears like a work of sculpture, the stony lips of lovers together forever. As a nineteen year-old, I'm fascinated with the couple. Why would two old people kiss like that? Are they trying to relive their youth? Are they trying to be younger than they are? Are they clinging to each other in this time of distress? Are they older lovers about to part? Are they former lovers who have just met again? Are they shutting out the cold misery of the times with the warmth of their lips?

While Podoske and I stand in the park, the air raid sirens begin their sad song. Even before they die out completely, a German buzz bomb approaches low over the tip of St. James Park, cruising over the buildings, trailing its ungodly sound, a pulsing, popping staccato-like rhythm, a knee-weakening, testicle-wrenching sound. Painted a dull gray, it heads almost toward us, closer and closer, its motor still running.

"Hey!" shouts Podoske. That damn thing's coming right at us!"

"There's not much we can do about it. Just hope it keeps moving."

"If it's engine even sputters, I'm diving in the ditch!"

Almost overhead it speeds toward the west. We look up in frozen horror at its stubby wings, its bottle-shaped pulse jet motor on top, its cruel pointed body crammed with explosives. In London they have a saying about the buzz bombs, "Praise the Lord, and keep the motor running." To our great relief, the weapon passes over, but several miles past us its motor quits, followed by a dull, earth-shaking explosion.

We'd finally seen a German buzz bomb up close, much closer than we'd wanted. Now we understand what the British have been enduring. They streak across the channel anytime of night or day, landing indiscriminately, always destroying a random civilian target. A few plunge to the earth with their motors running while some glide for miles after their motors quit. Others angle straight for the ground. It is their unpredictability that has Londoners on edge. They try to keep up their spirits, but they are uncomfortably wary of the menace. A cartoon in the paper depicts an Englishman going about his business in the usual way, but the artist has drawn one of his ears much larger than the other, a huge ear, always tuned for the slightest sound of a buzz bomb. Gathering our wits, we move on, now fully understanding why our "Noball" missions are so important.

Hoping to avoid the expense of the Mayfair dining room, we scout around town for other restaurants. We get a good meal, equivalent to 80 cents in our money, at a place called Ala de Roche. Almost all of the menus, mostly at swanky places, are printed in French that means nothing to us. The waiters always have to translate it for us. Some of the waiters are French. One of them is angry because we don't like his dessert. We just nibble at it, and give up. It's a mixture of berries and celery and other unidentified ingredients without sugar.

The train back to the base is even more crowded than the one we had ridden to London. Passengers rudely push themselves onto it, butting their own bodies into the others to make room. Some charge with their suitcases, using them as battering rams. In this situation the British are the most aggressive people I have ever seen, bodies against bodies like a football scrimmage, cursing, groaning, grunting and yelling. But in order to get back to our base on time, we must act as they do, except we try to use a little more tact and grace.

By the time we board there are no seats left, most of us just looking for enough space to stand in. I shoulder my way out to the vestibule at the end of the coach where several other soldiers and civilians stand. The hollow clatter of the wheels on the rails, and the squeaking and binding of our car against the next one create a mild din, but at least the space is airy and not so crowded. Standing among the others in the vestibule is a young British woman, somewhat shorter than I am. She has a pleasant face, and seems very open. She looks carefully at those around her rather than staring out of the window, hanging her head or looking at the wall the way preoccupied people do. I'm drawn to her openness and gentle smile, as she seems to peer directly at me. She wears her dark hair pageboy style with straight bangs across the whiteness of her forehead. Her blue eyes sparkle subtly, and when she smiles broadly, she reveals a tiny gap between her two front teeth, a feature that somehow becomes her.

"Hello," she says. "How did you like London?"

"Oh, fine. It was my first time there."

"It can be confusing if you haven't learned the streets. Did you get to see Westminster Abbey and Parliament?"

"Yes, I was very impressed."

"Where are you going now?"

"Just back to the base near Peterborough."

"Oh, it's nice there isn't it? Have you seen their great cathedral?"

"Yes, once. It's hard to believe there's so much space inside."

"What part of the States are you from?"

"California. I'm a long ways from home."

"Well, we really appreciate what you Yanks are doing for us over here."

I enjoy our conversation, especially because she's attractive and sweet sounding, and I'd just been around men for so many months. She listens attentively to my every word. I see only her face as the countryside flies by the window in an amorphous blur.

At Northampton the train slows for the station. She looks at me and says, "Well, this is where I get off. Why don't you get off the train with me?"

Before I have a chance to think, I reply, "No. I can't do that. I've got to get back to the base before my leave expires."

She turns slowly, and says, "Very well then. It was nice talking to you. Goodbye."

She steps out onto the station platform, and soon disappears in the crowd, leaving the vestibule suddenly empty and cold.

I think about the woman all the way back to the base. Did she really like me? Was she so fond of me that she wanted to be with me longer? Was she attracted to me? Or was she merely a prostitute on her way back from London? Perhaps she'd been with the others at Picadilly. I'd heard about British women who marry American soldiers, hoping they'll be killed so that they can collect on their insurance money. Was she one of those? She hadn't given me her address. If she were really sweet on me, she would have done that. Or did she expect me to ask her? I realize I will never see her again or ever know what her true motives were, and perhaps it is just as well.

Being in London, except for the buzz bombs and the mobs of soldiers on leave, had given me the chance to draw back from the grim business of the war. The flying of missions that had consumed me before, had been pushed into a remote corner of my mind by the two pleasant days away, but as the train nears

Peterborough I begin to think about what lies ahead. I'd flown only 11 missions, and suddenly the rest seem almost insurmountable. I know there will be an end to it all someday, but I don't allow myself to think about it.

THREE DAYS OVER MUNICH

Drawn curtains still hide the mission map as we gather in the briefing room. We had returned from our leave in London only two days ago, and now, reluctantly, begin the grim business of flying missions again. Briefing is like attending a stage play, except that until the curtains part, we have no idea what the nature of the drama will be. Still logy from sleeping and tense about where our assignment might take us, we talk softly or joke nervously, waiting.

When the briefing officer finally pulls the cord, the map looks as though they had used nearly a whole ball of red yarn to mark our route deep into Germany. We hadn't flown there since our bombing of Hamburg nearly three weeks ago, a raid that I had thought briefly might be my last. Our target today is Munich in the far southeast corner of the country, a flight that will keep us over enemy territory for more than five hours. We become silent and pensive as the captain explains the details. They've attempted to plan our route away from charted flak areas, but he tells us we can expect strong opposition over the target.

No one is happy. All of us know there will be losses. The attack will be a maximum effort of over 1000 heavy bombers from the Eighth Air Force in England and the Fifteenth Air Force based in Italy. Our own best chance of survival will be the multitude of planes taking part. German gunners can neither shoot nor hit all of us, the statistics being in our favor. They mean little, however, to the crews that are shot down. American fighter planes will cover us all the

101

way into Munich and out, discouraging the Luftwaffe pilots who know that the odds will be against them.

We go to our airplanes stoically, climb inside them with an air of resignation, busy ourselves with our tasks, and hope for the best.

Carrying eighteen 250-pound bombs, some with delayed fuses, and full tanks of gasoline, we take off into the English morning. We climb through the overcast, losing ourselves in its milkiness, then break out into the clear, a soft white sea of clouds spreading out beneath us.

By the time we reach Felixstowe on the east coast of England, we fly at 15,000 feet. Like silver dragonflies, planes extend out before us and trail behind, gleaming pulses pushing southward and eastward, and I among them, and with them, and in a sense shielded by them. The morning sun beats on the clouds, whipping them into creamy white blinding layers. I put on my sunglasses against the glare.

Shortly after passing the enemy coast, a tangle of high clouds cuts us off from the lead and high box. By the time we emerge from them, we can no longer see the rest of our group. Dangerously alone, we attach ourselves to another formation with square "G"s on their tails, receiving permission to proceed to the target with them.

Around noon, still a solid deck of clouds beneath us, we approach Munich. Bursts of antiaircraft fire over the city are so thick they merge into a pocked layer of blackness. The barrage is like the one described by the veteran back in cadet training—"Flak so thick you could walk on it."

Beneath the bruise-like smear two specks twinkle, each one glinting lower than the last, bombers going down, their wounded aluminum bodies twisting and flashing in the sun.

Knowing that we must pass through this shrapnel storm is psychologically numbing. I slip on my steel helmet, encase myself in heavy flak jackets. We close in on the target. I'm still alert, but in the grip of a teeth-clenching, asshole-tightening air of resignation, as though I've temporarily suspended my life, immersed it in a deep freeze.

I work the bookmark from the tightness of my pocket, the cloth one with the 23rd Psalm printed on it, the one Edith, my Aunt Mary's friend, had given me when I had been home on leave. I rub my gloved thumb over the tiny green embossed words then mutter them behind my oxygen mask. "The Lord is my shepherd; I shall not want." I finish the prayer, leaving out not a single word lest the prayer should falter. I stuff the bookmark back in my pocket, silently repeating the important part—"Yea, though I walk through the valley of the shadow of death, I will fear no evil, for thou art with me." As calmly as possible, I commit the protection of our plane and my body to God.

I check my intervalometer and switches, making sure that all is ready for the correct bomb release when the moment comes. Flak begins bursting around us like ugly black popcorn, but the German gunners, apparently hampered by the same cloud layer that interferes with our bombing, set up a general barrage rather than tracking us. They appear to throw up as much flying steel as possible into a large space, hoping to snag some of us.

The lead plane opens its bomb bay doors; the rest of us do the same. The flak becomes more intense. Smoke markers from the group ahead arch down toward the target, leaving dirty white trails that drift in the wind currents like the long bloated bodies of snakes. With the thick clouds below, Norden bombsights are useless, the job being taken over by PFF equipment, radar that can penetrate them. Not as accurate, but adequate. Bombs begin to float out of the belly of the lead plane. We drop ours, the combined loads briefly filling the sky beneath us. The lethal missiles streak through the clouds like a flock of vengeful ducks, but we'll never see the explosions, never really know where or what we hit.

We bank sharply to the right, soon breaking free of antiaircraft fire. The long trip home begins, all four engines humming without any obvious flak damage. I'm relieved that all the bombs had left their shackles smoothly, as we'd been warned not to bring back any of the delayed fuse bombs. On the way into Munich enemy gunners at Brussels, Karlsruhe and Stuttgart had taken pot shots at us, but our route home would take us south of that path.

Our objective at Munich, had we been able to bomb visually, was the destruction of the industrial area near the heart of the city, particularly those factories involved in the production of rocket-propelled and jet fighter planes, potentially a major threat to our air force. Our radar target had been the center of the city, the objective ostensibly being the main railway station and marshalling yards. This had been a different type of mission as all our others had been directed at specific military targets. Aiming for the center of the city makes me uneasy.

By the time we reach the Dutch islands, the time is1500. We begin to let down immediately over the channel, flying at only 7000 feet by the time we reach the English coast. We all feel the indescribable relief of returning, our oxygen masks off, breathing normal air again like ordinary human beings.

* * *

We're dumbfounded at briefing early the next morning when the parting curtains reveal the same target as yesterday. The planned route in and out is almost identical. The combined air forces had lost 36 planes over Munich yesterday, a small number compared to the hundreds of bombers that had flown the mission, but the toll becomes even more significant when we think that 360 men just like us didn't come home. Again, we're to attack the industrial area, but if clouds cover the target, as predicted, the center of the city will again be bombed by radar.

We take off rather late at 1030, nosing into the soft gray oblivion of the overcast until we break through the tops at 6000 feet. Today each plane carries four 500-lb general purpose bombs and six 500-lb incendiary clusters, the intent being to blow up the buildings then set them on fire, the magnesium incendiaries being almost impossible to extinguish. Today we fly in the high box.

Still weary from yesterday's marathon mission, we face another eight or nine-hour flight. Once on our way, heading out over Felixstowe at 16,000 feet and climbing, the whole venture seems like *deja vu*. Over the Dutch islands, now at 21,000 feet, we head almost south then dogleg to the east toward Munich, gradually climbing to our bombing altitude of 27,000 feet. Even the clouds appear the same, the brilliant sun beaming off of them as though it's a great soft snowfield.

Squadrons of P-47 Thunderbolt fighters fly nearby, looking silvery against the pristine blue of the near-stratosphere. We feel secure when we see them. P-51 Mustang fighters will replace them when we near the target. The P-51 pilots are lucky in a sense, flying far above the flak while we must fly through it.

Even the bomb run is much like yesterday's, the sky over Munich again dark with flak. Today their fire is more concentrated and accurate, the black blossoms blooming all through our formation. We fly by the old puffs and into fresh ones, cave-black and writhing against the blue sky. Huddled in my flak jackets, my steel helmet heavy on my head, I again suspend my life. I pray silently and tend to my job, making sure the bombs will be released properly. Sometimes I wish I didn't see so much, my Plexiglas bay window affording me a "front row seat" on the whole sordid drama. Better to be a radioman, staring at his radio, fiddling with the dials, listening to the chatter or a navigator peering into the fluorescent green "safety" of his G-box screen. I must keep my eyes on the lead plane.

Shortly after the bombs fall away, Lt. Irwin's plane, near us in our formation, drops out after being hit by flak. He heads downward, briefly rights his plane then loses control, the crippled bomber twirling into a flat spin as it falls. Only three parachutes appear, but perhaps others had delayed opening theirs. Losing one of our own is always sickening, not the moment it happens, but later when we think about it, knowing it could just have well been us.

Minus one airplane and with most of our box's planes damaged but still flying, we emerge from the flak. Our plane appears, at least, to have not taken any major hits.

Every mission is a macabre roulette game. We give the great wheel a spin, hoping that the clattering ball will not land on our number. Even though I pray for protection and give God His credit, I know in my heart that anyone's survival is a matter of chance. I'm sure that some of the men on Lt. Irwin's crew had also prayed.

As before, we dump our bombs on the center of Munich using PFF equipment. Although my first thought is for my own safety and survival in wading through the flak, I feel uneasy about dropping bombs on the city center, even if there are railroad yards or scattered industry there. The mission verges on leveling a city or trying to attack a legitimate target without being concerned about civilian damage. We may have bombed churches, beer halls, hospitals, schools, department stores or apartments where innocent people live, most of them caught up in an evil not of their own making. I find myself hoping they'd all made it to underground shelters.

We had bombed Munich at 1330, immediately banking to the right, and streaking for home. The plane next to us, one of its engines damaged, has trouble keeping up with the formation. Not wanting to be left behind, a predicament that could prove fatal, the crew throws out everything they can to lighten the load. Out go their flak suits and helmets then long strings of machine gun bullets twisting toward the earth. By shedding the equipment, the pilot, using his skills, manages to stay in formation. Three hours later we reach the channel, finally landing at Polebrook near 1800.

Exhausted, we eat supper at the mess hall, then crawl into bed where we all die away into a sound sleep.

* * *

With our limbs still leaden from our two exhausting missions, orderlies arouse us in the dark for another. We stagger around in the dim light of the barracks, the eternal questions on our minds.

"Goddamn it! Where to now?"

"This is the third day in a row that we've had to get up at this ungodly hour."

"We've gotta get some rest. I'm still exhausted from yesterday."

"We short of crews or something?"

"Shit, I've had it!"

"I can hardly get out of the sack."

We're all disheartened at briefing when we see the same lousy mission on the board. Some groan aloud, some growl under their breaths. The target at Munich must be extremely important. Apparently two days of bombing through the clouds with over one thousand bombers had not destroyed the factories. We had caused terrible fires yesterday they tell us. Intelligence reports that the Munich fire department had to call in fire fighting equipment from as far away as Augsburg and Stuttgart to help stem the flames. The Eighth Air Force alone had lost twenty-four planes on the Munich raid yesterday, bringing our two-day losses to forty-four.

We carry the same bomb load up through the perpetual English overcast, emerging from the tops at 5000 feet. We fly in the lead box today. Again flak is heavy and accurate over the target. Today they not only fire a barrage, but also track us, their shells exploding all through our box, nipping at us. So much shrapnel flies that it peppers all of our planes. Lt. Aldrich's plane takes a hit in the oxygen system. Without it they must dive quickly to a lower altitude. Alone now, and plummeting toward the clouds, he asks for fighter protection. He finally disappears into the clouds below, his chances of making it back quite slim.

Again we had bombed by radar, but a momentary break in the clouds reveals that we had probably overshot our target by about a mile.

An hour after bombing, flying the beginning leg of our journey home, about twenty-five FW-190s and Me-109s attack our low box head on then turn back to pick off stragglers. All of this happens behind us so I can't see it. For some reason our friendly fighter cover has been lax today, the Luftwaffe taking advantage of the lapses. I look down to see an FW-190 attack the rear of a formation flying about 1000 feet beneath us. The German pilot approaches from the rear and below, barrel rolling and firing his guns as he climbs. He eventually stalls then falls off into a power dive straight down toward the clouds, his plane becoming a black speck before the clouds engulf him. One B-17 at the rear, hit by the fighter, begins to fall back, two of its engines leaving long trails of thin white smoke. With two engines down, he can't keep up. Falling farther and farther behind, like a wounded animal unable to stay with the herd, he is prime game for Focke-Wolfe predators.

Another FW-190 flies level, out to our left and up, far out of range. He appears to be flying along with us at our speed, probably radioing our altitude and direction of flight, our absence of fighter cover. He has undoubtedly mentioned the smoking B-17, now alone and vulnerable, and ready to be finished off. I turn my chin turret toward the fighter, fixing his small dark silhouette in my neon-tinted reticle. Warren, the navigator, peers into the G-box, not seeing anything. I swing back, brushing his padded shoulder with my gloved hand. When he turns to me, I point out the fighter, hoping he will be ready to man his guns. Finally the fighter veers away. We keep our formation tight, our wings tucked as closely as possible.

We fly back slightly south of our inbound route, a path that takes us dangerously close to the flak batteries at Kaiserlautern, Brussels, Karlsruhe, Antwerp, Ghent and Stuttgart, all of the places firing at us without much accuracy. Antiaircraft fire at Brussels sends a B-17 from another group down in flames.

We also had become separated from our high box on the way home, losing some of our support. Later, as we fly through thick cirrus clouds, our formation becomes even more scattered. Three of us, finding ourselves separated from the box and alone, look for another group to join for protection. As we try to attach ourselves to one group, it becomes obvious that the gunners don't trust us. They point all their guns and turrets directly at us. Even after contacting them by radio, they are wary of us. We think the gunners have been told to keep their guns on us for a while, just in case—that if we should make any hostile move, they should fire.

I'm uncomfortable with their weapons trained on us. What if a nervous gunner imagines that a gun has been turned on him?

Most of us had heard stories, probably based on fact, that the Germans had captured B-17s intact. They had flown them near a group, claiming they were lost. Once the group had let them in they'd opened fire on the unsuspecting crews. That's why the men on the planes next to us are nervous.

For what seems ages, they have us in their sights. I think to myself that it's bad enough to fly missions and escape enemy fire without facing the irony of being shot down by our own forces. We are careful to stow our guns so that they will not be alarmed.

After looking down the muzzles of their guns for an eternity, they finally relax, having been convinced that we're friendly. As their armament turns away from us, we breathe much easier.

Even in a game as deadly and insane as war, there are rules of combat. Some acts are considered low and cowardly, others decent and honorable. A captured B-17 joining a group, then firing upon it, is considered despicable, an act that demands retaliation.

We had heard a story, undoubtedly true, that a B-17 crippled by fighters and anti-aircraft fire, had lost altitude over Germany and was considering landing at one of their airfields. When interceptors flew along side at a safe distance, the bomber pilot lowered his landing gear, an international signal that the crew had given up and wished to land. Seeing that the bomber had lowered its landing gear, they flew closer to escort it to the nearest field. At that point the gunners of the B-17 opened fire on the fighters, shooting down at least one of them, a dastardly act that broke the rules.

Several days later, in retaliation, the German fighter squadron surprised this bomber group, attacking them in England just as they entered their landing patterns, when they thought they were most safe, destroying a number of the bombers.

We finally reach the Dutch coast and begin our descent over the channel. By the time we reach mid-channel, clouds and rain showers swirl around us, forcing us down low to get under the clouds. We skim over the deck, the rain driving against the Plexiglas, creeping across it in thin lines of quivering water.

Ducking in and out of showers, we finally land at Polebrook shortly after two in the afternoon.

Eight of our planes had been damaged by antiaircraft fire, including ours. Both our wings had taken flak holes, including our extra gas tanks which fortunately had self-sealed.

At interrogation, as Podoske, Johnston and Warren sip their shot glasses of bourbon, we all complain to the intelligence officer.

"We've flown to Munich three days in a row, and we're dead on our feet."

"Yeah, I know," says the officer, "Let's hope this is the end of it."

Today's mission had been our fourteenth, entitling us to wear an oak leaf cluster on our air medal ribbon, a tiny golden oak leaf no larger than a lady bug, small compensation for all that misery.

* * *

Next day I write a letter home, frustrated because I can't tell them what's really happening in my life. "I sure got behind on my letter writing didn't I? Once in a while you will have to expect not to get any letters. Sometimes everything comes at once…I am still in the best of health, and as fit as a fiddle, although a little weary."

THE TEXAN

The Texan's bed is directly across from mine, on the other side of the barracks. A co-pilot, he and the other officers on his crew had been assigned to our squadron shortly after I'd finished my early missions. I liked him right away because of his gentleness and soft-spoken manner. His hair is so thick and wavy that he can hardly keep it combed, giving him a slightly wild look. He peers through squinty eyes, the kind that so many Texan men have. They always appear to be looking out over the vastness of the plains, the sun burning into their faces. Most of us are clean-shaven, but he cultivates a sparse moustache that looks like a teenager's effort to appear manly. He's short, about my height, and speaks in a high-pitched voice twisted by a twangy accent. Although he's friendly and open, I soon discover that he prefers to keep to himself, a trait that makes him difficult to know.

Most of us complain about having to wait for trucks to take us out to our planes, and we are especially cranky about hanging around them for sometimes up to an hour after a difficult mission, hoping for a ride in. The hardstands, dispersed widely over the field for protection against enemy bombers, are so far away that we can't walk in carrying our flying equipment, flak suits and machine gun innards. Fed up, the Texan claims that he's going to make his own conveyance. He announces that he's going to build a steam turbine-powered vehicle in the base machine shop that will take him to and from the plane any time he wants.

Some of us scoff at him, skeptical that he'll even try.

"Y'all don't believe me? Just wait and see."

During spare time between missions he's often missing from the barracks. True to his word, he works diligently in the repair shop fashioning his machine. One day he walks into the barracks, proudly carrying some of the parts he's made, beautifully machined assemblies that he says will function in the steam turbine system. The polished metal gleams and clinks in his hands, each piece fitting snuggly and cleanly into the other. I'm impressed with his professional craftsmanship, but he has many problems to solve. How will he construct a boiler? What will he use as fuel to heat it? I think he's a dreamer, an eccentric who only dabbles at a project rather than seeing it through.

The days go by, but we see nothing of his masterpiece. He finally confesses that he's going to give up on the turbine.

"I know what to do, but I can't get all the materials I need. I have other ideas though. I'm sure I know how to make my machine. Y'all just wait. I'll build it."

I respect what he says, but dismiss his latest idea as just another dream.

In less than a week there's a whining sound outside of the barracks as he rides up on his new scooter. The contraption uses two old tail wheels salvaged from B-17s and the motor from a Sperry ball turret powered by a storage battery located under the seat. It's a remarkable piece of equipment. I'm intrigued; amazed that he could conceive and construct it. He beams with pride.

The high-pitched whirring of his scooter is often heard as he darts around the airbase. His only problem is that he must recharge the storage battery frequently to keep it going. He's made a believer out of me and has won my admiration as a skilled, possibly brilliant machinist. I change my perception of him from eccentric to clever.

* * *

Close to three o'clock in the morning, an orderly stomps into our barracks with his flashlight, shattering our dreams. In the hazy limbo between sleep and waking, we listen for our names as he reads off the crews who will fly. "Breakfast at 03:30, briefing at 04:00," he shouts as he leaves. He calls all of us.

As some struggle out of bed, begin to dress or leave for the latrine, the Texan sits bolt upright in bed, his eyes heavy with sleep, his mop of hair tousled, the shadow of a beard on his face. He remains in the same position as though he's frozen, catatonic.

"Come on Tex," says his pilot, "Get up. We're gonna to be late."

With anger in his narrowed eyes, he stares across the room.

"There's no goddamned way that you can finish your missions," he shouts, his voice loud enough to be heard through most of the barracks. "Its hopeless! If they don't get you one day, they'll get

116

you the next! There's just no way you can make it without being shot down sooner or later!"

We continue dressing as he babbles, but we listen, knowing that there's a subdued element of truth in what he says. Those around him gently encourage him to roll out of the sack and soften his comments. A pilot tells him that it just seems hopeless because he's half asleep. At first I think he plans to sit there and never move. He seems immersed in a trance. He might possibly refuse to fly, an act that would ground him for good. His pilot treats him with understanding.

"Come on Tex. It'll be okay. We need you."

Gradually he emerges from whatever state he's in. He stops railing and begins to slide out of the covers. He dresses silently, still preoccupied, acting as though he slips into his flying suit for the last time.

I'd never heard a guy talk like this before, although I'm sure that many of us had harbored the same thoughts to some degree, choosing to keep them to ourselves. I think his tirade reminded us of our own anxieties, ones that we keep buried, having glossed them over with layers of hope and optimism. Planes may go down, but we shall always return. None of us ever talk about our fears to each other, deciding instead to live with them, locking them up in the privacy of our minds, each man dealing with his own kind of demons. The Texan had let his escape.

I had no idea that he suffered from such deep consternation, that he was gripped by such terror on his missions. Perhaps the hours in the machine shop, working on the various models of his scooters, had kept his mind occupied, had kept his dark thoughts at bay. His anxieties may have helped him produce his wonderful scooter.

Later the familiar mosquito-like buzz of his marvelous machine is heard as it dashes through the darkness. Perhaps the flow of cool morning air on his face will freshen his outlook, push his fears far down into the depths of his mind where they may rest.

THE VILLAGE

Cruising over a blinding ocean of clouds, we once again head for Munich. I slip on my sunglasses against the glare. It's the same monotonous mission; even the clouds seem identical. I feel suspended in the hypnotic drone of the engines, the blue vault of the sky, the vast featureless shelf of mists stretching out endlessly below us. I resign myself to the long hours ahead, the discomfort and the waiting. I have ample time to think about the Munich air defenses, their black bath of shrapnel.

The formations begin to leave long contrails behind them, thick white lines etched against the deep blue of the sky, swirling plumes coalescing to form an imitation overcast dense enough to cast gray shadows beneath them. From my great bubble of a window I watch the mesmerizing drawing of vaporous banners and the swarms of silver ships that create them. We had been rousted out of bed in the dark, had taken off at 5:30 in the morning. I'm already weary.

The clouds become higher as we swing toward the southeast, filmy walls of cirrus, dense and deep. We climb to 28,000 feet to get over the layers, but they slope up even higher ahead. The group in front of ours attempts to penetrate the barrier, undoubtedly hoping to break free on the other side, but then suddenly begins turning back. Our planes, in order not to tangle with them, turn in a wide circle in the clear air, waiting for them all to emerge.

Our group leader finally decides to attack the secondary target at Stuttgart, hoping for better weather.

We bank to a more easterly heading and drop our altitude nearly 2000 feet.

In the confusion of vapor trails, altered plans and weather, another group bears down on our new target from a different angle, putting us on a collision course. We quickly abort the bomb run, again curving away in a broad 360 for another try. Clouds still blanket the target. German gunners bracket us with a loose barrage, their fire inaccurate, but intense enough to damage our planes. The lead pilot reports that our radar bombing equipment is inoperative, so some of the boxes bomb on the smoke markers left by other groups.

Our box of 12 planes flies on with its bombs, seeking a target of opportunity somewhere out in the clear. We fly toward a large marshalling yard, strings of tiny freight cars lining the maze of tracks. Our bombs float down silently. The rail yards erupt like a volcano with flashes and brown mushrooming clouds of pulverized earth and debris. Tank cars carrying gasoline or oil gush great orange tongues of flame that merge into a pillar of jet-black smoke.

Shortly afterward, as I glance off to the side, I see a single plane from another group drop its bombs. I watch them explode in a trail down the main street of a small village, undoubtedly blowing out all of the storefronts and every window in town, probably killing people who had felt relatively safe in their non-military town. I would like to think it a careless mistake, but the bombs had exploded in an even trail about 100 yards apart, as though the pattern had been intentionally set up on the bombardier's intervalometer. I find myself hoping it had been a colossal accident.

The sight bothers me. I don't understand why he couldn't have waited to jettison his bombs in the English Channel, but blowing up anything anywhere in Germany seems to be sanctioned.

I think the incident a natural for the Nazi propagandists. "Cruel Americans Bomb Peaceful Village. Innocent Women and Children Killed." I had heard German news broadcasts in English back in the barracks. They often reported that British or American planes had attacked their churches, always full of women and children.

We let down over the channel, flying at only 5000 feet by the time we cross the English coast at Clacton. Scattered clouds float over the green crazy quilt of peaceful fields. I'm relieved about being home safely once again, but the disturbing vision of that German hamlet stays in my mind—the small town wrapped in soft haze, the ugly brown geysers erupting down its main street, my imagination supplying the deafening explosions, destruction, the cries of people.

PEENEMUNDE

Our engines throb as we gradually gain altitude over the North Sea. Their parts work harmoniously—sparks setting off confined explosions, lubricated pistons pumping in their cylinders, fuel feeding precisely—four Pratt and Whitneys humming and blending like a fine quartet.

I turn to the side window and look out at the silvery blur of the propellers pulling us up toward the edge of the stratosphere. The discs of the whirling blades remind me of dragonfly wings, that same filmy delicacy.

Nearly two hours lie ahead before our formation will reach the enemy coast, plenty of time to mull over the possibilities, the likely reception that awaits us. Our route for now keeps us well out to sea, away from flak batteries and German fighter bases. Clouds dapple the ocean's face, almost cover it in places, but the deep blue of the water peeps through the breaks. After so many missions to Munich in southern Germany, flying north over the sea is a relief and much safer.

Our target today is Peenemunde where Nazi scientists have established a large rocket experimental station. Far ahead of America in the development of these weapons, they have already perfected a sleek missile, the V-2 (Vergeltungswaffe-Zwei or "revenge weapon number two"), capable of being arced hundreds of miles to a target. Within the past month the V-2s have begun to terrorize London. They fall out of the stratosphere without warning, devastating whole city blocks on impact. Some of the V-1 buzz bombs can be stopped with antiaircraft fire, pursuit planes or barrage balloons, but there is no defense against this one.

By 0830 the enemy coast close to the German-Danish border slips beneath us. So far, there is no opposition. Once past the Danish Peninsula the Baltic Sea comes into view, its surface dimmed with haze. Bits of the large Danish islands of Lolland and Falster appear through breaks in the clouds.

To the north where it is clear lie the flat checkerboard fields of Sweden, still neutral in the war. I gaze longingly at that sunny patchwork. A number of damaged bombers on previous missions, unable to fly back to England, had fled north to its airfields and sought sanctuary. Those crews were out of the war, none of them ever having to face the dangers of bombing missions again. Rumors are that some had flown there with weak excuses in order to avoid further combat. Others flying in southern Germany had flown to Switzerland, also still neutral.

Turning south, we head for the rocket facilities. I still think about Sweden. What if our plane should be severely damaged today, and we should have to limp over there? What a holy relief it would be.

Flak gunners put up their usual barrage near the target, painting the sky with a scattering of dark puffs until they join into an oily smudge, a gauntlet that we must fly through. A break in the clouds allows us to bomb visually in the final moments of the run. Most of the antiaircraft fire bursts both below and above us, catching the low and high boxes, but leaving us relatively free. They had also concentrated most of their fire on the group in front of us. Roulette again, unpredictable chance seeing us through.

Our 500-pound bombs bracket the target, an electrolytic hydrogen plant and a steam power plant.

After "bombs away" we bank sharply to the right, scurrying toward the safety of the Baltic again. Our group is still intact, none of the planes damaged so much that they can't keep up.

Following the same path back over the peninsula, we once again cruise over the serenity of the North Sea. We gradually lower our altitude. I feel my body begin to unwind. Within two hours we'll be home. The exhilaration of completing another mission, our 16th, washes over me like a warm breeze. In the emotional glow, finishing all of them and going home seems possible, even probable. I bask in an aura of childlike optimism.

Eventually our group crosses the English coastline, flying at only 1000 feet under a low overcast. The countryside, even though dulled by murky clouds, looks like heaven to me.

MY REAL LIFE

On our way to the base theater, Podoske and I stroll along the damp, well-worn path through the woods. We watch for occasional puddles and patches of oozy mud grooved with the marks of bicycle tires. Sometimes we'd ridden our own bikes here, but it's more pleasant to walk. Ancient oaks and beeches spread their canopies over us, the lacy layers of leaves and branches blocking much of the sunlight, preventing the trail from ever drying out completely.

Walking here is peaceful, the gnarled limbs enfolding us in a protective tenderness that, for a while, separates us from the world outside. At times I've longed to wander through the trees by myself, far away from the tensions of flying. Podoske and I stand aside as two other men bound for the theater pedal by. After they pass we move on, talking to each other.

"I got a letter from Eleanora today," says Podoske.

"She's really special to you, isn't she?"

"She's it as far as I'm concerned."

"I have girls who are friends, but no real girlfriends. At least they write to me."

At the far edge of the woods, near the theater, we come to an old manor house owned by a wealthy family. Our airfield is on a portion of their vast holdings. We don't know if anyone lives in it now or whether it's being used for military purposes.

We find a pair of empty seats in the Quonset hut theater, most of the men having arrived before us. Their babble and laughter ricochet around the curved walls as they wait for the movie to begin. Cigarette smoke layers itself in a bluish haze. Several men in the back have blown up condoms then tied the tag ends so that they look like large white balloons. They bat them toward the front, the next rows, grinning and laughing, swatting them up each time they settle in reach of their outstretched hands. The ghostly inflated rubbers bounce around the room like colored balloons at kids' birthday parties; the men, I suppose, reverting for a few moments to nurture the child that is still in each of them.

Podoske and I are excited about the movie, *Two Girls and a Sailor,* starring June Allyson, Gloria DeHaven and Van Johnson. With her blonde hair, laughing eyes and angelic face, June embodies the woman that I and probably every other man here dream about. Like the forest we'd just passed through, she takes me away from the war, but more importantly, she connects me to my other life, my real life. Once engrossed in the film, I'm transported out of the present. A parade of American performers floats across the G.I. screen—Jimmy Durante, Jose Iturbi, Harry James, drawing me back to my roots, back to the theaters of my hometown.

I enjoy any movie that takes me out of myself for a few hours, but I don't like those about Nazis or combat anywhere in the world, any film that places me in my present life. We often laugh at the propaganda that saturates many of them.

Since so many productions had been shot in Southern California, I'd often caught fleeting glimpses of home, places that I recognized. I'd written home—

"This evening we went to the post theater and saw the Marx Brothers in *Go West*. It was very silly, but enjoyable. A lot of the scenes on the railroad were taken on the line running from Oceanside to Escondido, that old Santa Fe Line." Once I'd seen the Inglewood station in a movie. Each time I identify a spot in California, I love it. It makes me homesick, but for a brief moment I'm connected.

* * * *

Our squadron's not flying today. Some of the other crews are, but it's our turn to stand down in the rotation. I sit on the edge of my bed, my tablet on my knee, ready to write a letter home. I head it up the way I always do, "Dear Mom, Pop, Charline and Pal." Charline is my sister, Pal my dog. As usual, I can't tell them very much—only about my health, the movies we see at the base, washing out my underwear. Mainly I respond to the news from home, the stories from Inglewood that flow through their letters.

My existence now is contrived and unnatural. We are men thrown together temporarily for a specific purpose, the bombing of an enemy. I bond with my crew and some of the men from the others, but that camaraderie arises out of simply being together, working as teams and sharing common and often harrowing experiences. I relish the adventure of being in a foreign country, seeing new sights, but the interest in it is so tainted by the war that the thrill of it is largely lost.

My other life lies thousands of miles away, and centers upon those I love—my mother, father, sister, relatives, neighbors and church and high school friends, all of whom are a part of who I am. It also revolves around the familiar sights and sounds that are meaningful to me—the wind in the casuarinas trees, snow on top of Mt. Baldy, the whistle of the noon train, the first rains of the season.

Writing letters and receiving them is my only link to that life. I'm hungry for any news about home, no matter how trivial. I write—"Yes, I would like to get the Inglewood paper. If you could possibly send it, I wish you would. Even the advertisements mean something to me over here."

My mood varies with the number of letters I receive. At times I get none for three or four days, dampening my spirits, making me feel strangely alone. On other days I garner a half-dozen, and my spirits soar.

I read them over and over, absorbing the news—Charline's physics exam, her graduation from high school, the death of my Great Aunt Laura, whom I had loved, my grandmother staying a few days at our house, receiving pictures of Senior Dress-up Day at high school, Charline entering nurse's training, repapering the rooms at home, getting rid of the chickens out back, having a supper in the backyard barbecue enclosure, the heat and the brushfires burning in the foothills—all of the items vital to me.

As I write the letter, squadrons of bombers assemble for a raid, their thunder shaking the earth, their vibrations rippling through my body. As the rumbling begins to die out, I hear an oscillating screaming of engines, the wavering death cry of a bomber spinning out of control, lower and lower, ending in a muffled blast. It's several miles away. We don't even go outside. "Oh, God," we say. "Somebody went in. I wonder how it happened?" It's silent in the barracks for a long time, and for a while I stop thinking about home where my real life is.

A FIRST ENCOUNTER

Cruising at 25,600 feet, we fly our third mission in four days, all deep into Germany. My bones ache with fatigue and tension. After the raid to Stuttgart only three days ago, I fell asleep on my bunk with my clothes on and slept that way the remainder of the night. I've never felt rested since. The heavy steps of the orderly with his quivering flashlight had rousted us from our beds about 0400.

Aloft for three hours, mostly over enemy territory, our formation nears its objective. German gunners had taken potshots at us in three different places on the way in, most of their fire inaccurate.

We close in on the IP, the point at which we turn toward the target for the bomb run. Our plane is in the lead box today, each of our twelve bombers loaded with 500- pound bombs to be dropped on the Messerschmitt aircraft factory at Augsburg. The high and low boxes carry 100 pound incendiary clusters to set fire to the rubble that we plan to create. It's a bright sunny day in Augsburg, with scattered cumulus clouds floating peacefully in a clear but hazy sky.

Suddenly the intercom crackles. "Tail gunner to crew. Bandits coming in, 6 o'clock high!" German fighters had never directly attacked a flight we were in since I'd begun flying missions, but now the vibrations of our machine guns from the top turret ripple through our bomber. The tail gunner and ball turret gunner blaze away. I see nothing but the superb summer day in Augsburg, all of the action happening behind me. "I got one!" yells Stanowick in his high-pitched voice. "I got one too," claims Lucas, the engineer and top turret gunner. "Two of our planes are going down!" The intruders damage the plane next to us, but not mortally. I feel helpless—not seeing—not being able to do anything about it—just waiting and hoping that the fighters miss us with their cannon shells and machine gun fire. It's like expecting to be shot in the back, being suspended in time, anticipating the impact.

The attack is over in minutes, our crew and aircraft unharmed. But we'd lost two of our Polebrook planes in a few lightning seconds.

According to the gunners, a half-dozen Focke-Wulf 190s had flown above our group masquerading as friendly escorts. They'd then peeled off out of the sun, surprising the tail end of the high box first—sleek silver-gray fighters with bright orange wing tips. The two bombers from our field, flying at the rear of the formation took the brunt of the attack, both going down instantly, one exploding, the other spinning down out of control and on fire. Only two parachutes had billowed out into the freezing air. Even though I can't see any of the action, the carnage is easy for me to imagine—the thick orange flames and black oily smoke.

Radio reports warn that several other groups are fending off enemy planes, creating a great deal of confusion just as they begin their bombing runs. Once again there has been a lapse in our cover, the Luftwaffe picking up on it immediately. When our formations are exposed, the German pilots seize their opportunity, inflicting as much damage as possible before our escort spots them. Had our P-51 Mustangs been with us, they never would have attacked. The German Air Force, smaller than it was in the past, but still effective, flies only when the odds are in its favor.

The group directly in front of us, dogged by enemy interceptors, fails to turn toward the target, so we slide in ahead of them. As usual the Germans saturate the space over the target with anti-aircraft fire. Within the barrage other flak gunners track us with six-gun salvoes. Our bombing results are marginal, most of our explosive power only grazing the edge of the Messerschmit factory.

The flak is fearsome, but our box, the lead, is spared the worst. Our plane, in spite of the fighter attack and the shrapnel, hums along undamaged. It is difficult to understand how or why it is. Or is there any "why?" Did the silent prayers do it, or was it the roll of the dice, the spin of the roulette wheel?

We fly toward the northwest, aiming for the Dutch islands, particularly Oberflaake where we'd entered the enemy coast, still hours away. On our way out, flak gunners fire at us near Stuttgart and at Breda in Holland where we turn sharply to the north to avoid their barrage.

Finally reaching the island, we begin to let down, our mission essentially over. I've laid my flak suits and helmet aside and look forward to being over the security of the English Channel and beginning the euphoric sweep back into England. Seemingly out of nowhere bursts of flak begin to explode all through our formation. I quickly retrieve my protective jackets and helmet, snap on my chest chute. We'd encountered no antiaircraft fire here on the way in, but German intelligence must have calculated that we would leave the continent at the same place we'd entered, as this was common practice. They'd apparently moved in a number of mobile anti-aircraft batteries to surprise us.

They track us accurately, as though they know our exact route and altitude. The soot-black puffs pop among us for what seems at least ten minutes, inflicting more damage to our already riddled formations. Miraculously our plane avoids a damaging hit.

Out of range now, we lose altitude over the channel, settling in towards England. Nosing into a soft layer of clouds, we briefly lose ourselves in its milkiness, then fly low underneath.

After landing we learn that many planes had been damaged not only over the target, but also over the Dutch islands. Nearly half of our planes have suffered battle scars. Many men had been wounded in the surprise barrage over the Dutch islands, one tail gunner blinded, perhaps for life. I emerge from it all unscathed, and again I don't know why. I'm whole, and everything functions, my skin smooth and unblemished, not even scratched.

The following day I write home, "I can't seem to get many letters written these days. Don't worry though, I write every chance I can get. We have been working very hard, and about all we can think of is the sack (bed). We haven't had much sack time for a while—until last night. Boy was that wonderful. I think I had about twelve hours of sleep, and I mean solid sleep. I'm still in good health, and my morale is satisfactory. I do sort of pine for home though. That is the one thought I have in mind; getting home."

THE IMPORTANCE OF BALL BEARINGS

Nearly every airman had heard about the infamous raids on Schweinfurt months before. Heavy flak and relentless attacks by German fighter planes, many of them lobbing rockets into the B-17 formations, had nearly decimated our then smaller air force. On August 17, 1943, 36 bombers had been shot down out of a force of fewer than 300 unescorted planes, and on October 14, 60 had been lost. Newspapers had carried headlines about the carnage, and Life magazine had presented a full spread with paintings and diagrams explaining the air battle. B-17s had fallen like hapless ducks on the first day of hunting season. The Germans had suffered great losses also.

When the parting of the curtains in the briefing room reveals that Schweinfurt is today's target, a wave of gloom ripples through us. Just the name "Schweinfurt" packs an emotional wallop. Ball bearings are essential to all German war machines, and most are produced there. If we eliminate their production, we essentially destroy the tanks, trucks and mechanized equipment that will use them. It 's their Achilles' heel. The Germans, of course, also understand their importance and go to great lengths to insure their uninterrupted manufacture. The plant will be well defended. Thinking about it sets our jaws and quiets our voices.

The tides of war have changed over the months, our situation today being quite different from the days of those earlier ill-fated raids. There were fewer bombers then and more German interceptors. Today, hundreds of bombers will attack, wave after aluminum wave of them. American fighter planes will escort us going in, over the target and coming out, the Luftwaffe not daring to attack unless there's a break in the cover. But the specter of Schweinfurt, and the memory of what happened there hangs over us like a foul odor.

We take off at 0730, nosing up through a solid overcast until we emerge at 6000 feet. We're part of the lead group of the first wing over the target today. Shortly before 0900 our formations enter the continent over the Dutch islands, then fly toward the southeast and finally nearly due south to avoid the heavy flak batteries at Cologne.

The stretched-out might of the 8th Air Force is pasted against the intense blue of the high-altitude sky. Several antiaircraft batteries had fired on us on the way in, but the gunners were largely off the mark.

It 's 1000, two and one-half hours into the flight. We bank abruptly to the left, toward the IP, still nearly thirty minutes away. I ready my flak vests and helmet, check my chest chute, go over my intervalometer settings. Each plane carries five monstrous one thousand-pound bombs, enough explosive power to twist the girders of the ball bearing factory into steel spaghetti. Only fifteen minutes away now. I know the gunners will saturate the space over the plant, filling it with as much flying shrapnel as possible. I pray quietly.

Near the IP, the point at which we turn toward the target, a high cloudbank slopes up in front of us. Slowly climbing over the fibrous mass, we reach

28,000 feet before riding over the top. On the lee side, descending, our squadron settles through thin cirrus layers, flying just beneath the clouds at 25,000 feet, our bombing altitude.

A smoke screen set up by the Germans on the ground partially obscures the plant, but the sky above it is perfectly clear, not a single burst of flak marring it. Usually the area over the target is black with antiaircraft fire as they shoot at groups ahead, but today, as yet, their guns are silent. Being the first planes over the target is eerie, and I'm on edge. I know that it's just a matter of moments. I can almost feel the gunners tracking us, waiting for the perfect time to begin shooting. I find myself wishing they'd begin. The anticipation of the barrage is unnerving.

Our bomb bays are open; the long doors swung downward, the icy wind tumbling around the massive bombs. I concentrate on the lead plane flying next to us, waiting for the lead bombardier to drop his bombs. Still no flak.

Just at the instant of release, black blasts thump all around us, the sooty smoke puffs writhing then fading into gray smudges. The artillerymen below had waited patiently, all of them firing at the optimum moment. Our bombs float away, thirty tons of them from our box alone, sinking down through the purity of the air. Unceasing heavy flak bursts among us, riddling some of the planes, but failing to knock any of them down. Our strike straddles the target. I imagine ball bearings scattering all over the countryside.

The gunners give up on us as we bank sharply to the left, preferring to concentrate on the next group.

I 'm always relieved and somewhat amazed when we fly through such a mess and come out whole. All four engines hum perfectly, and no one on our crew is hurt. How many times would we get away with it before the law of averages catches up with us? Although some of our planes are damaged, all fly well enough to maintain a tight formation.

Speeding toward the northwest, again avoiding the guns of Cologne, we head for the Dutch islands and the channel. Unlike the lapses in cover during our last mission, our fighter protection had been perfect today, the Luftwaffe apparently deciding not to chance an attack.

By 1245 the coast at the Dutch islands passes beneath us, our exit at the same point we had entered them, the flat blue sanctuary of the English Channel spread out deliciously in front of us. Suddenly flak begins to explode all around us, obscuring our peaceful view of the channel with ugly black blotches. Once more we'd been set up, the Germans calculating that we'd again leave the islands through our entry point, just as we had on many missions before. They'd been waiting for us, had over four hours to bring in and set up their mobile guns and tracking equipment. They dog us with their accurate fire, damaging two of our planes so severely that they drop out of formation and limp home on their own. Just as had happened on the mission before, some of our men would be wounded. The gunners follow us with their fire, nipping at us until we are finally out of range.

Inside my cocoon-like wrappings of flying clothes and armor, I smolder with rage. I'm not angry with the Germans who are cleverly doing what they are supposed to do, but at our mission planners who constantly route us out over our entry point. I think about these men, these high-ranking officers who live in manor houses and assemble at strategic headquarters where they plot raids in complete safety. They deal in statistics, targets and results without understanding what an airman experiences, without any real feeling for him. Losses of men and planes are only numbers to them, their only concern being arranging for their replacements to keep the groups at full strength. I had neither met a mission planner nor been inside of a planning room, but my imagination supplies all of the details I need to stoke my anger.

Complaining gets us nowhere. Many of us had expressed our concerns after German fighters had jumped on us during the Augsburg raid, that we needed to fly in 18 rather than 12-plane boxes so that we'd have more concentrated firepower, especially when flying deep into Germany. We continue to fly 12-plane boxes; the command assuming that our fighter cover is enough to protect us. But there are sometimes lapses in fighter cover. What then?

Our tires squeal on the runway at close to 1400. It had been a long, harrowing, exhausting mission. Thirteen of our planes had been damaged by flak, five of them severely, but we had all eventually returned to the field. Now Schweinfurt had become a part of our history too.

LONDON AGAIN

Even if the train is jammed with soldiers and civilians, I'm glad to be on my way to London again, away from the airfield. I watch the peaceful countryside go by, the quiet soothing greenness of it. Johnston, Warren, and Podoske are with me. We have nineteen missions behind us now, enough to make us feel like veterans.

At the railroad station in London, we queue up for a cab, and then ride together to the Mayfair Hotel where we'd stayed on the previous trip—really the only hotel we know about. As before, I room with Podoske, and Johnston with Warren.

After languishing in the luxury of our hotel room, we set out to explore the city again. Even though Podoske and I had walked miles on our first trip, we'd not been able to see all the sights. Map in hand, we join the crowds on the sidewalks and head for Buckingham Palace. I admire the grandeur of the old place, but its cold, gray stony look depresses me. We stroll through Hyde Park and around Serpentine Lake, ending at the Queen Victoria Monument.

Exhausted from our long hike, and ready to sit, we find a movie that we'd wanted to see, *Going my Way,* with Bing Crosby. I think it quaint that the British call their movie theaters cinemas. Engrossed in the film, we rest our weary legs.

We go to a French cafe for dinner, a place we'd liked on our last visit, A La Broche. We think it's the best place in London to eat, at least from our limited experience. The waiters must have taken a liking to

Podoske and me because some of them who waited on us last time greet us warmly in their broken English.

"The next time you come in with your other two friends, we'll fix something very special for you."

"That'll be swell. We'll talk to them about it."

The waiters and most of the patrons are French. I enjoy the rapid lilt of their language, all of it sounding strange and mysterious to me.

Podoske and I are bushed by the time we go to bed, dropping off to sleep immediately. Earlier in the evening we'd heard the mournful wail of the air raid sirens warning that buzz bombs were on the way. Some had plowed into other areas of the city. Podoske had seemed uneasy.

A tremendous explosion rocks us out of our sleep as a buzz bomb slams into the neighborhood no more than a block or two away. The concussion shatters nearly every window on the opposite side of the street from our hotel, the broken glass tinkling down the sides of the buildings, the shards falling musically, like the simultaneous motion of hundreds of wind chimes.

Podoske leaps out of bed, flicks on a lamp, fumbles for his shirt.

"What are you doing?" I ask, surprised.

"I'm not gonna stay up here. It's too dangerous. That bomb was too damn close! You can stay if you want, but I'm getting the hell out of here!" He hurriedly thrusts his legs into his trousers.

"Where are you goin' to go?" I ask him.

"Down to the basement."

"How're you goin' to get any sleep down there?"

He straightens his uniform and says, "I don't know. I'll find some place. I just know that I'm not gonna stay here." He lights a cigarette, and disappears, slamming the door behind him.

I can't sleep, my mind too busy playing with the idea of what might have happened had the bomb struck closer. A surge of adrenaline prepares me for action rather than sleep. I look up at the dark ceiling, thinking. I know that it's dangerous staying in the room, but the nasty missiles are likely to fall anywhere, and London is a huge place. Perhaps Podoske is overreacting, but his leaving disturbs me. I wonder about where he's going to sleep. The hotel bed is comfortable and luxurious compared to our Spartan sack back at the barracks, and I'm tired. I decide to take my chances.

Just before I drop off to sleep, the air raid sirens howl again, like packs of wolves baying at the moon. In the silence following the warning, I hear it, the unmistakable staccato of another one of Hitler's playthings cutting through the night. It becomes louder and louder, sounding as though it will fly directly overhead. I decide that if the motor continues to run, I'll stay right where I am. I listen intently. The motor stops. I bound out of bed faster than Podoske had, dash for the door, and crouch in the hallway next to the wall. Podoske might have had the right idea. The low drum roll of the blast echoes through the streets, the detonation probably a half-mile away.

The all clear sounds as I crawl back into bed, hoping that it'll be the last attack of the night.

Podoske raps on the door in the morning. He had merely dozed on a chair in the basement. His eyes look heavy and swollen.

After going to another cinema showing, *It Happened Tomorrow,* with Dick Powell and Linda Darnell, we meet Johnston and Warren for lunch, this time at the Mayfair. They all order drinks. I choose cider off of the list because I'd had it at home, and it had been nothing but apple juice. When the waiter serves the drinks, he puts down a small bottle with a cap on it in front of me. The liquid inside is clear. What I'd had at home was amber. I check the label to confirm it. I decide that that's just how they make it in England. The cider fizzes slightly, and doesn't taste right, not nearly sweet enough.

Our food arrives as we talk and finish our drinks. Suddenly my face flushes. It heats up as though I'm embarrassed, and I feel light-headed. They laugh at my pink cheeks, even harder when I tell them I'm dizzy. I'm drinking hard cider, alcoholic stuff, and I have a buzz on, much to their delight. Being a teetotaler, I'd never experienced the sensation before, and I don't like it. I stop drinking, gradually letting the strange feeling subside.

Later, I walk by myself near a park when another V-1 races across town. Its motor stops, and, not knowing for sure where it is, I hunch down near the closest brick wall in the park. I huddle on the ground, waiting for the impact, wanting the blast to be over no matter where it is, wondering whether I'm safe. It finally explodes several miles away with a dull ground-shaking thud.

A few hours later I sit in a barbershop. The gentleman cuts my hair with great flourish, a metallic snapping of scissors, most of the time snipping only the air. The mournful sirens begin to moan again. The barber becomes jumpier, complains about how awful these buzz bombs are. Then both of us hear the motor. He leaves me, scuttling to the door to check. With his hand shading his eyes, his scissors still in his other hand, he scans the hazy sky over the buildings. He returns, telling me that it appears to him that it's passing to the south of us. The erratic, insidious weapons make nervous wrecks of most Londoners.

At the railroad station, I mill around with the rest of the crowds, trying to board a train back to Peterborough. They are all so packed now that it's really difficult to travel. I've never seen people fight so hard to scramble into the coaches. The clamoring looks uncivilized to me—all those bodies pushing, shoving and cursing. I don't make the first train as I refuse to shoulder and elbow my way in. The next time I stand by the train door early and just let the crowd push me in.

I sum up my attitude about our trip to London in my next letter home. "We had a swell time, but I don't think I will go there again until those buzz bombs stop. They just about got us last time, and the same thing this time. We risk ourselves enough on duty without doing it on a pass. Those things are no joke. I'll tell you about them sometime."

THE DISBANDED CREW

He stands outside our barracks window with his slate-gray .45 pistol pointed directly at the officer inside. In attempting to appear calm and casual, his quarry moves slowly around his bed, adjusting his clothes, arranging them in drawers, but he wears the pale mask of fear. The bill of the gun-wielder's cap shades his face so that I can't see his expression, but his seriousness is set in his stone jaw. Both men are at the far end of our barracks, their voices indistinct and muffled. Their anger, rather than erupting into harsh words or shouting, smolders. The officer outside, the co-pilot of a crew that had just been broken up, because, it is rumored, they had violated flying procedures, keeps the barrel leveled on the man inside, never wavering. Except for the movies, I'd never seen anyone point a weapon at another person.

I think it strange that the gunman hadn't walked into the barracks. Why does he stand outside and talk through the open window? He doesn't appear to be drunk. He stands erect, almost at attention, always steady. I listen to his controlled voice, his hurling of soft-spoken accusations, but I can't make out his words. The quarry inside talks back to his accuser, again in subdued tones, as though he speaks under water. Their actions produce a quiet yet intense drama. It is as though I'm viewing it through a gauze screen, like a faraway shadow play.

It appears that the co-pilot blames the officer inside for the break—up of their crew, as though he had some part in "turning them in." I don't know; I can only guess.

I sit on my bunk not knowing what to do. Interfering with their argument might be dangerous considering the constrained intensity of it. A boiler seems about to explode. I also don't want to be in the line of fire should they suddenly shift their positions. I remain on the bed, worried that I'm about to witness a murder that I can't prevent. Their distant quarrel goes on and on, or so it seems. They remind me of two dogs circling each other before they hurl their bodies together. I'm ready to drop to the floor if shooting begins. Only a few men are in our barracks, apparently feeling as helpless as I am, fearing we might precipitate a catastrophe if we should approach them.

Finally the officer inside convinces the co-pilot to put his gun away, but the puzzling conflict goes on. All of us have .45 pistols and ammunition. We carry them with us on missions so that if we have to bail out over enemy territory, we can protect ourselves from outraged citizens. The thought of using my pistol to settle an argument would never occur to me, but this dangerous fellow has no such inhibitions.

Eventually, after hurling some final threats, the man outside walks away. I don't know for certain what the conflict had been about. The drama had floated into my life for a brief time then drifted away without my understanding of what I had seen.

* * *

Streaking over the treetops, the silver P-51 Mustang buzzes our field, its engine screaming at top speed. It flashes by the control tower, hurtles down the field, turns, then comes back again, this time on the deck, only a few feet above the runway. Swooping up at the end of the field, it banks sharply, its silver wings glinting in the sun. Racing back toward the field again, the pilot flips it over on its back. It drops low, still upside-down, its rudder pointed to the runway, down, down until it's only a few feet off the ground, the tail nearly touching, its engine whining at full throttle. Remaining in the same position, it gradually lifts over the trees, rolls over, and is gone, disappearing over the farms and hedgerows.

I'd watched the spectacle with open mouth, thinking the pilot extremely skillful or foolhardy or both. His reckless intrusion was against the rules, and surely he'll be reprimanded. The rumor is that the flyer is the pilot of the same disbanded crew as the barracks gunman. His assault on our base appears to be in retaliation for his release, a paying back for the damage done to his ego. It too might be his way of demonstrating his skill in front of our commanding officers.

I don't know how he commandeered the plane. Perhaps he'd been reassigned to a fighter group, but his actions will surely embroil him in deeper trouble.

The buzzing Mustang had been another drama shrouded in mystery. It had happened in front of my eyes, the silver vision of the speeding plane, the shrieking of its engine, yet I don't understand it.

I walk away from both actions with a hazy story woven out of facts, rumors, guesses, hunches, imaginings and impressions. The prevailing tale is that the crew hadn't taken their break-up lightly. It had injured their self-esteem, unleashed their deepest emotions, opened up rivers of revenge. I, like a man in an audience, had just witnessed two acts of an absurd play, yet I know only traces of the truth.

TEA ON THE RUNWAY

My vision of them lasts for only a moment. As we slowly lift off on our way for a raid near the French coast I look down upon the men, workers huddled on the opposite runway. They form an instant photograph, a snapshot of British workman on the tire-streaked concrete having tea. They clot around a small portable stove with a teakettle on top. Most have stopped working and stand talking to each other, the old men bundled in their coats against the cold overcast, their European caps pulled snugly over the tops of their heads.

I think about how quaint it is, how British it is to have afternoon tea, even on a wind-swept runway in the middle of a vast grassy field.

As I look down on them, I also think about how fortunate they are. They'll sip their hot drinks, work a few hours longer, then go home. They're not anxious about their lives; they are in no danger. They may be exhausted, even bored with their work, but they're not afraid.

We, on the other hand, must be concerned about ourselves, worry about whether we'll be able to return to our "home." For a moment, in a brief lapse into self-pity, I yearn to trade places with any one of them. I'll sit on the chilly cement ribbon, nursing my tea, letting it run warmly down my throat, adjusting the bill on my cap, waiting the few hours before I can go home to my hearth and my familiar bed. You, whoever you are, can take my place.

In my imagination I see them watching us rise from the runway with our burden of bombs. "There they go again," they say. "They're off on another raid. Well, we're too old for that. But if I were young again, I'd be glad to be in their shoes—those men rushing off with their vigor and fine bodies. If I had my youth back, I'd take my chances."

MUNICH AGAIN

After the luxury of our two-day pass to London, we're right back at it, on our way to our perennial target, Munich. I would think that with all the tonnage dumped on the city during our previous three raids, there would be nothing left to hit.

We'd taken off late, about 1030, nudging up through a low gray overcast. The sun is straight overhead now, beaming down on a white wasteland of clouds that hide the green hills, dark forests and tidy villages of central Germany. With the ground cut off we might be anywhere in the world. The flight will be long and tedious. Munich still lies an hour away.

I adjust my oxygen mask. It has become slippery from the condensation of my breath inside. The rubbery smell of it is repulsive. I try to think about the good times that Podoske and I had in London, in spite of the buzz bombs. But I concentrate more on my upcoming week's leave in Scotland, the time off, called a flak leave, given to us after our 20th mission to calm our nerves and give us the strength to finish the remainder of our tour. Going north to the land of the Scots seems like a dream to me—a whole week on our own, sleeping, traveling and eating at our own pace, free from rude early morning interruptions and away from danger and tension. Podoske is going with me. I get along well with him, both of us being fond of exploring new places.

As we near Munich, we begin to leave contrails, thick persistent ones that draw long wooly lines across the pristine blue sky. I don my armor and check my bomb settings. Just beginning to feel the apprehension of flying through the flak, I ponder the eternal questions. How intense will it be? How accurate? Will this be the day we lose our gamble, or can we get away with it yet again? Each plane carries ten 500-pound bombs, some general purpose and others incendiary. A few have long delay fuzes so that they'll explode after a deep penetration or, more cruelly, blow up later, preventing rescue workers and firemen from doing their job.

We begin the bomb run. Today our position is in the high box next to the lead plane. The sky ahead is dark with a hellish pall of antiaircraft fire. I mutter my usual silent prayers, feel an acute looseness in the bowels. I yearn to be back at the base, sitting on the safety of a toilet seat. In my imagination I picture the latrine there, peaceful and quiet, in soft shadows, hear sparrows chirping in the shrubs.

Dense rounded clouds still obscure the ground, but here and there, small breaks give us momentary glimpses of it. Again our bombing will have to be done with radar, not nearly as precise as visual sighting.

Flak bursts all through our formation, most of it catching the low and lead boxes. Our bomb bays are open, the doors spread out like a flapped incision, exposing our insides. The Germans send up a general barrage, filling a predetermined space with as many exploding shells as they can pump into it.

After dropping our loads, we bank sharply to the left, soon escaping from their fire. I don't think we've been hit, always a miracle to me, but the planes lower in the formation have surely been riddled. We head for home, all of us able to maintain formation.

By the time we reach the channel we've dropped to 20,000 feet. We descend steeply, finally able to rid ourselves of our oxygen masks and cumbersome flak vests. After turning in a wide circle, we sink softly into a solid cloud layer, losing sight of the world for several minutes. Breaking through underneath at about 1000 feet, we fly below the overcast to Polebrook, landing at close to1700.

Ten of our planes had been damaged by flak, minor skin punctures for the most part. As the radar on our lead ship had malfunctioned over the target, the bombardier dropped his bombs on the smoke markers of the group ahead of us, the long arching trails that plunge to the target with the bombs and then drift with the wind. Intelligence officers determine by photographs showing bits of the ground through breaks in the clouds, that our bombs had fallen three and one-half miles northwest of the BMW plant at Allach.

I 'm exhausted.

CHARLES N. STEVENS

THE RETURN OF THE LANCASTERS

Even around machines of war like the B-17s, the dew on the grass still smells fragrant. I stand outside our plane on the hardstand, breathing in the freshness of the morning, waiting until the last moment to grab the edge of the small hatch under the nose to catapult myself inside. The sun still hovers below the horizon, spreading its pale gray-blue light through the eastern quadrant of the sky. Except for my inner thoughts about the mission we are about to fly, the morning is peaceful and still.

The whining drone of British Lancaster bombers, returning one by one to their airfields after night raids over Germany, breaks the stillness of the morning. In the dim light they are small silhouettes, winging overhead toward the west. The peculiar wailing of their in-line engines is different from the solid roar of our radials. For some reason I like the sounds of the Lancasters—lonely plaintive tones like melancholy singing.

Unlike the British, we fly in daylight, a tactic they think is too dangerous. The Lancasters fly off singly into the night, each plane being a raid in itself. The pilot must fly the plane, the navigator must get it to the target, and the bombardier, or bomb aimer as the British call him, must use his bombsight to deliver his load accurately. American bombers fly in formations, three boxes of twelve planes each for every group, all at close but slightly different altitudes. Only the navigator in the lead plane of each box is in charge of finding the way to the target, the rest merely following along with their charts and G-boxes. The British bomb singly, each bombardier being responsible for hitting the target, but only the bombardier in the American lead plane is in charge of locating the target and using the Norden bombsight. The rest of us bombardiers, like automatons, open our bomb bay doors when he does, and drop our bombs when he does, thus creating a wide pattern of destruction below, saturation bombing. We release them by flipping a toggle switch—like turning a light on or off at home. We have intervalometers we must set to space our bombs, but we do not have bombsights. All of us had been highly trained over months of grueling flying and endless study to master this instrument. We had all been accurate and accomplished enough to win our wings and receive our officer's commission.

I'm disappointed that I'm not performing what I had been trained for. I'm what some call a "toggleier", a "glorified gunner" throwing a switch when I am "told" to.

With over half our missions completed, I had asked Johnston, our pilot, what he thought about our becoming a lead crew. His answer had been immediate and definite. "I told you in the States when we first met at Alexandria, that my goal was to finish my missions as quickly as possible and go home. We all agreed to that, and I still feel that way. If we were a lead crew, we wouldn't fly as many missions, and it would take us a hell of a long time to finish. I don't have any ambition to be a lead pilot."

He clearly cares neither about being heroic nor having the honor and responsibility of being a lead pilot. His interests are at home, his future life, reestablishing his baseball career or going into business.

The situation is different with pilots. They had been trained to fly heavy bombers, precisely what they do in combat. Bombardiers had been trained to use the Norden bombsight, but they never use it in combat unless they are lead bombardiers.

If I pursue the idea of becoming one, I would have to leave our crew, men I had trained with and flown with for so long that it seems I have known them all of my life. They are good men, and I am comfortable with them. Johnston is a superb pilot, and I have great confidence in him.

Even if I should attempt to become a lead bombardier I might not succeed as many others also covet the position. Perhaps the debacles of my first two missions, whether I was to blame or not, would always be a mark against me.

Why does it matter? I can never get that vision out of my head—that film clip that I'd seen in the Newsreel Theater downtown before I'd ever worn a uniform. I had slouched in my seat, watching a motion picture of a British bombardier aiming through his bombsight, dropping his bombs squarely on the target. I believe that in the darkness of that theater with the light from the screen flickering on my face, I had quietly made up my mind. I'd decided that if I should join the Army Air Corps, I would become a bombardier, just like the one in the film. All through cadet training I had wanted to be that man, and it now appears I will not. I back off from my boyish dream and accept reality.

But what should I tell my parents and friends whom I suspect hold the same expectations that I do? If I don't bomb the target with a bombsight, what good am I? What a disappointment I will be to them and to myself. How will I handle their questions when I get back home? I shall certainly not bring up the subject. I might give them vague answers. I already feel slightly humiliated, shy and a trifle ashamed when I think about their possible questions. In a strange way, after all of the terror and tension I have gone through on our missions, I consider myself inadequate for not being able to live up to that exalted vision of myself, for not being what I set out to be.

I'd been caught up in the flimsiness of my own dream. What does it matter anyway as long as I return home alive? Johnston is right. Let's get the job done as quickly as possible and get back to our real lives in our hometowns.

But I look up at the small singing silhouettes of the Lancasters as they fly out of the dawn, wondering how their bombardiers had fared, whether they had hit their targets. I put faces on them, each man looking like the British bombardier in the newsreel—that heroic soul who in spite of enemy fire had guided his bombs to the target.

I silently salute them then hook my hands around the escape hatch, throw my legs inside, and pull myself up into the plane.

ON LEAVE IN SCOTLAND

"It's no use. Follow me, boys!" says the conductor, in a hurry, clipping off his words. We try to board the Edinburgh train at Peterborough, but with all the seats taken, and the aisles and vestibules jammed, getting on the coach is impossible. Podoske and I trail behind the uniformed trainman as he strides toward the baggage car. "This is the only place we can put you," he says as he slides open the heavy door. "It'll do," we say, thanking him for allowing us on board. As there are no steps, we pull ourselves up and throw our legs in, a tougher job than climbing into a B-17.

Podoske and I had wanted to go to Scotland, but we had no idea that the trip would be so difficult. We settle down in our austere accommodations, both of us sitting on the hard floor, leaning up against a large wooden box marked "R.A.F." Several other boxes and a number of bicycles take up some of the space in the car, but there's plenty of room left. A small bulb in the ceiling provides just enough light to see. Alone in the baggage car, we press our backs against the hard container and try to relax. It will soon be dark. This car will be our bed and lodging for the night, the train not due into Edinburgh until early in the morning.

Later we try to close our eyes as we listen to the steady rhythm of the locomotive just in front of us, and the hollow rattle and swaying of the baggage car. I can't sleep. I doze off only briefly, the sounds sometimes seeming far away. As the train comes to a halt the door slides open, and several other people struggle up to the floor. At each station stop, from then on, other passengers join us, all of them seeking out space where they can sit or stretch out. Some are civilians, but others are British soldiers and sailors. Most of them are polite and quiet, the majority simply wanting to find a place to sit or sleep.

After midnight still more climb aboard at unknown places. They talk to each other in a language I don't understand. It finally dawns on me that they're actually speaking English, but in a Scottish dialect or accent, heavy on the r's and replete with cut-off syllables. I'd never heard anything like it before.

The growing number of passengers with their strange talk fades in and out of my consciousness as I try to doze. Some scuttle out of the car at station stops, returning quickly with mugs of tea, steam curling up from them, catching the feeble lights of the station through the open door. Even though I'm half asleep, the scene fascinates me—the travelers scattered over the floor among the boxes, in every position, some nodding off, others miraculously asleep. Some huddle in coats, a few wrap themselves in small blankets. Everyone, in spite of the conditions, seems kind and considerate.

By the time we chug into Waverly Station in Edinburgh, the sun is up. Heavy with fatigue, Podoske and I slither out of the baggage car and look for the city. As the station is at the bottom of a large gully, we must trudge up a steep stairway to find the main part of town. We finally discover a Red Cross Service Club that had taken over an entire hotel on the main street of

Edinburgh. Lodging for one night is four shillings or about eighty cents in our money. They offer clean beds, hot showers and a nice place to eat, the meals costing two shillings six pence, about fifty cents, cheaper than any meal in a restaurant.

We immediately hit the sack, hoping to make up for our lack of rest during the night.

Refreshed at last, we walk out to explore the town. Our first view of the city disappoints us. Edinburgh, in spite of its reputation for beauty and history, looks drab and dead, its stone buildings dull and gray. A steeply sloped park borders one side of the main street, the other side walled in with large shops and hotels. Every double-decker tram in the city rolls past our hotel, their rattle and clanging echoing through the streets. At the base of the hillside park is the railway station where we had arrived earlier. Edinburgh Castle perches on a cliff opposite the station, a massive stone reminder of another age.

We wander around the city, not always knowing where we're going. We walk through narrow streets where girls make kissing sounds at us from doorways and windows. Most of the kissers we don't see, their phantom puckering seemingly emanating out of nowhere. We plod straight ahead, paying little attention to them. Past the Hollyrood Castle we come out into the open at Queens Park. I look up at the green grass-covered slopes and bluffs, and suddenly feel that I'm in a book of fairy stories, the scene transporting me back to my childhood. The soft verdant hills are the very image of the pictures that I had admired so much in the children's books I had read many years before. I gaze at the hills, feeling the fusing of two distinct periods in my life. The illustrations that had seemed so fantastic in the books have now become solid and real.

* * *

After exploring Edinburgh, we board a train for Glasgow where we arrange for a room at another Red Cross hotel. Once settled in our quarters, Podoske and I start out on foot, letting the sidewalks take us where they will. The city appears larger and much grimier than Edinburgh. After decades of coal burning, soot had worked itself into every stone pore and stuck to every surface so that each building wears a dark patina. Some buildings appear as black as charcoal. We walk down the gloomy streets wondering how the people can bear to live in such a dirty place, but they stride by it as if the grit were not there. The creosote smell of coal smoke hangs in the streets.

As we amble about town, feasting on all the stimulating newness of a strange place, I have two general observations. The first is the number of banks we had passed, at least two in every block, more than I had seen in any other city. I had always heard about the Scots being very thrifty, so perhaps these are monuments to that characteristic. The second observation is that the Scots have more children than anyone else. Everywhere mothers carry babies or push them in prams. Hordes of other small children bound along the sidewalks or race through the side streets. Perhaps they are biological compensation for the loss of their young men in the war. The whisper of pursing lips and soft whistling again float out at us from young women standing in shadowed doorways or peering from windows.

The soot and dinginess of the city finally weighing on our spirits, we decide to board a bus to Loch Lomond, about twenty miles outside of the city. The idea of going to a place that's the site of a famous song excites us. "The bonnie, bonnie banks of Loch Lomond!" The vision of a lake that had only been a part of our boyhood imaginations would soon become a reality.

We find a seat on the top deck of an enclosed double-decker bus, a good place for some great views of the city and the country. Although the ride is smooth, the top-heavy bus leans precariously when it turns, especially on the winding road through the hills near the lake. Sometimes I think we're about to tip over, but the Scottish passengers seem unconcerned, as though the swaying is normal. Podoske is concerned, a worried look clouding his face. "This thing is going to fall over on one of these curves if that driver doesn't slow down. I'm about ready to go down below." Still upset, he sticks it out until we arrive at the lake.

The bus lets us off at the southern end of Loch Lomond. We gaze out at it, trying to reconcile the lake before us with the one lodged in our imaginations. I think it's beautiful, for Scotland, but I had seen much prettier ones in the United States. It's much larger than I thought it would be, and the rounded hills slope down gently to the shores, giving the whole scene a flatter profile than I expected. There are fewer trees, and the water is a lighter blue, almost a hazy gray. I'd been used to places like Lake Tahoe that nestle like blue jewels among steep-sided mountains covered with pines and firs.

We walk to the edge and look down into the clear water. Its freshness and purity makes us glad we're here, away from the tarnished cities and the war. Small boats cut through the water, and others rock in the wavelets close to us. In a shop I buy two souvenir handkerchiefs, one to send to Charline, my sister, and one to a girlfriend.

The leave is working. Our week off is officially called a rest leave, but everyone calls it a "flak leave" because we are all "flak happy", tense from having to fly through it all the time and hoping we'll make it. We've been able to get the war pictures out of our heads, and supplant them with those of new cities, new places and exotic scenery—supplemented with healthy doses of rest and personal freedom. The lakeshores are peaceful and still. We decide to return the next day.

On the way back to Glasgow Podoske refuses to ride up top. "You can go up there if you want, but I'm staying down below. I'm not taking any chances." I climb the steep stairs to the top deck because the view from up there is magnificent, and I have a passion for looking out of windows at the passing scene.

* * *

The following day Podoske and I stroll down a green, grass-covered hill with a full panorama of Loch

Lomond. Flocks of white sheep graze in the same field, but they don't pay any attention to us. I think about how lucky they are—just eating and sleeping and being with each other, not worrying about the war.

We reach the shore at the bottom of the hill then walk along the water, small glassy waves rippling and slapping at its shallow edge. Again we are truly on the "bonnie, bonnie banks of Loch Lomond," a fact that I must repeat to myself to believe. Telling my folks and friends about it when I return from overseas will be fun. I'll be the only one they know who has ever seen it, let alone walked its banks.

We struggle up another green hill near a large stone mill or factory. Suddenly young women appear at the windows, whistling and yelling at us as though they'd never seen men before. More and more of them poke their heads out of the windows, shouting and gesturing as though they are all a part of a comical puppet show. We wave at them as we plod up the hill, the women still agog at seeing two uniformed American officers leaning up the hill rather than the usual sheep.

And so ends the last day of our leave.

LIEUTENANT HIBBARD'S AIRPLANE

"Hey! We need you guys to fly right away. Hibbard's plane was shot all to hell, but they nursed it in to an emergency strip on the coast. We need you to pick up the crew," says an officer suddenly bursting into our barracks.

As we fly, I'm still trying to gather my wits. We'd returned from Scotland to find our barracks empty, all the crews out on a mission. The rumor is that they'd gone to Berlin. I'd been washing out some of my underwear in the latrine sink. By now the washing had dried, and I had just folded my shorts and socks neatly into the old drawers when the man burst in.

Warren and I spread our maps out in the nose of our plane as we angle up into the scattered clouds. Despite the mist, the sky is clear enough that we can use pilotage to find our way—comparing our maps with what we see on the ground. We fold them over when we find the correct sectors, the stiff paper crackling. We give Johnston a heading to an emergency airstrip on the east coast of England where Lieutenant Hibbard's plane, badly damaged after a raid over Germany, had to land.

Flying low over the green mosaic of English fields and the darker green clots of forests, we head toward the northeast. It had been a rough mission we are told, and we'd lost some planes. They'd bombed the Daimler-Benz plant at Genshagen, near Berlin and had caught the brunt of the capital's defenses. We'd missed the raid only because we were still officially on our rest leave. Had we returned a day earlier, we would have been part of the mission. Another spin of the roulette wheel.

As we near the isolated airfield, I think more about Hibbard. I'd always liked him and his whole crew, often talking to them near their beds in the center of the barracks. He'd been assigned to our squadron after we'd completed much of our tour. Handsome, of medium height, his hair thrown into orderly waves, he's gentler than most pilots. That air of self-importance that afflicts many of them is absent in him.

Hibbard has a wife back in Indiana where he had lived all of his life. I often chat with him about his state because he's familiar with all the places where my relatives had lived and where both of my parents had grown up. Always relaxed behind his benign smile, he is open yet quiet, friendly to everyone.

We finally spot the field, a lonely strip near dark cliffs that plunge down into the white-frothed sea. After circling in the fading afternoon, we settle gently onto the long runway. Hibbard's plane rests on the tarmac at the far end of the field. We taxi down an asphalt ribbon, parking next to his disabled bomber.

I'd never seen a B-17 so badly damaged. How the man had kept the crippled plane aloft, especially with the loss of engines, I don't know. Hundreds of small punctures riddle its skin. Holes large enough for a person to put his head through gape along the fuselage like painful wounds, the metal around them twisted and ragged. Pockmarks and tears gash and perforate the wings and tail. The ball turret guns are bent back along the tarmac, still pointing straight down, the position they had been in when the gunner had quickly evacuated. The plane must have trailed a plume of sparks when the gun barrels dragged on the runway during their landing.

I stand in awe of the battered Fortress and begin to imagine the agony and chaos that must have taken place inside as the crew dealt with their grim situation.

Lieutenant Hibbard and his navigator stand outside their plane, still shaken from their ordeal. As the navigator, a handsome young man close to six feet tall, attempts to speak to us, his lips quiver and his hands shake. He lights a cigarette with great difficulty. His deep brown eyes, dilated and glazed, peer at us beneath his dark brows. He appears to be a man who has seen his own death, then had been able to back away from it. His oxygen mask still dangles from his neck as though he doesn't know it's there. It saddens me to see such a fine, well-chiseled man reduced to such trembling.

Hibbard, pale and exhausted, tells us more about the mission and their escape. He speaks in a slow deliberate manner.

"The flak was deadly near the target, and a lot of the guys were taking hits. We lost an engine and began falling back out of formation. Everything was chaotic, and planes were going down. We couldn't hold our altitude. Once we dropped out, the fighters hit us. We lost our oxygen, and had to fly lower. We headed back toward England on the straightest course we could find."

Taking a deep breath, he continues. "After fighters made passes at us again, we decided to fly low to avoid them. I didn't think we could make it back, so I told the bombardier and the gunners to bail out. We were almost ready to jump ourselves."

He shifts his weight, his lips still pallid. "We decided to throw everything out of the plane we didn't need, then fly on the deck, staying away from cities. Since we were so low they shot everything at us from the ground, even 20 mm cannon. We started to lose our second engine. Either we were going to crash-land in Germany or ditch in the channel, if we could fly that far. By some miracle we found ourselves over open water, on our way to England. Somehow we got to this strip."

Before we take what is left of Hibbard's crew aboard our plane, I turn once more to look at their riddled relic, once a sleek silver machine. I find it almost providential that no one aboard had been hurt. I have new respect for the toughness of the B-17 and for Lieutenant Hibbard's skill in bringing it home.

Back at the base we learn more about the mission. Near the target, tracking anti-aircraft fire had pounded our group, especially the low box. On the bomb run and just after it, Focke-Wulf 190 fighters had slipped through our fighter escort, shooting down six of our Polebrook planes. Bombers piloted by Lieutenants Petty, Pattison, Barieau, Uttly, Boyd and Strange had been eliminated along with their crews in a matter of minutes. Sixty good men from our field had been lost. The barracks next door to us is nearly cleaned out.

That evening I look over at the empty bed where Hibbard's bombardier should be sleeping and think about his bailing out over Germany, imagining his legs dangling at odd angles as his parachute opens, wondering where he'll land and what will happen to him. He'd been a quiet man with a boyish face, and although I'd not known him long, I'd liked him.

* * *

The following day the base commanders reprimand Hibbard for his decision to have his crew bail out. If they'd made it to the coast, his superiors surmise, he should have brought them all back with him. He had had to make a choice among several alternatives, but the course of action that he had chosen had been flawed according to the higher brass. Now without a crew he's reduced from first pilot to a pool co-pilot, flying only when a crew is short.

I think the criticism of Hibbard is outrageous. He had to weigh his options in the heat of battle, at a time when his severely crippled bomber was barely flyable, yet he is judged by high-ranking officers who were not on the mission, who had arrived at their verdict from the comfort of their quarters.

Hibbard is shaken by his ordeal and the accusation against him. He mopes about and appears exhausted. Undoubtedly too, he's concerned with the fate of his crew who might have been killed, wounded or hauled off to prison camps. We let him know we are all for him, that he had done all he could do. Within a few days he is filling in as a co-pilot on other crews and is back in the air again.

HELPING MEN ON THE GROUND

Gaining slowly in altitude, our formation leaves the English coast at Little Hampton where we gradually turn to the right until we fly due south. Only a few small clouds freckle the face of the channel. During the past three weeks we had flown three forays into France in support of our ground troops—this is to be our fourth. We hope to brace a road intersection at Louviers with an avalanche of 100-pound bombs, each bomber carrying 38 of them in its racks.

Although we want to contribute to the ground war, our greatest fear is that, due to unforeseen circumstances—marginal weather, heavy flak or misidentification of the target—we might bomb our own men, a tragedy that would be difficult to live with. Tactical targets are sometimes very close to the front lines, and American planes had already accidentally bombed some Allied forward divisions.

* * *

On one such tactical mission, our first, we had flown to Saint Lo where we dropped tons of fragmentation bombs, weapons designed to scatter shrapnel in all directions, straight out and parallel to the ground so that they riddled vehicles and cut down soldiers. I couldn't help but think about the cruelty of it, men being struck down and wounded.

Our special instructions were the following: "Bombs must not be dropped short of targets. Targets are 1500 yards south of forward lines. Friendly artillery will lay down red smoke markers along north boundary of target at 2-minute intervals for 55 minutes." We were to bomb abreast rather than in our usual formations.

We flew at only 17,000 feet, but because of haze and a scattering of clouds the primary target couldn't be identified precisely. Flak bursts exploded widely around us, but hadn't interfered with the bomb run. Our box unloaded on a large road and an open field two miles away from the planned point of impact. Another box chose a target of opportunity 20 miles away, and the other, heeding the special orders, and fearing to make a mistake, decided to bring their bombs home after making two unsuccessful runs. We hadn't done much good for our troops.

By the time we reach the French coast midway between Cherbourg and Le Havre, we've climbed to 20,000 feet, our altitude for today's raid. Only a few puffy clouds float over the French fields, so we should be able to bomb visually. We encounter no enemy fire as we move inland from the coast, but I arrange my flak vests anyway, just in case.

* * *

Our second attempt to come to the aid of our forces was even more of a fiasco. We'd been assigned to ground support in the Saint Sylvian area. Although little opposition was encountered on our first tactical mission, the Germans were relentless on our second. Taking advantage of our low 14,000 feet altitude, they pointed every field antiaircraft gun they could find at us, lobbing shells into our formation constantly, their accuracy deadly. Because of the intense flak, some groups changed course, causing a great deal of confusion, a number of formations cutting in front of others.

During the bomb run the lead ship in the lead box was hit by flak, injuring half their crew, including the pilot. In the jabbering and excitement over the intercom by the wounded men, the bombardier thought he heard someone say, "Salvo!" Thinking it was the voice of the Air Commander, he dumped his bombs, the rest of the eleven bombardiers, on seeing his, dropping theirs. They fell miles off the target in fields near St. Germain du Crioult, luckily away from Allied troops. Our box and the low one had withheld their bombs, returning to the base with them. Over half of our planes were damaged, but all returned—with nothing accomplished.

* * *

Now some thirty miles into France, circling gently to the left, we head for the IP, our objective nearly twenty minutes away. Our increased altitude will work to our advantage when the flak begins. In a few moments we should be able to spot the knotty twists and turns of the River Seine.

* * *

Our third tactical mission, a more successful one, was to blast gun emplacements at Brest with 500-pound bombs. Antiaircraft fire was minimal, and the bombing results were good, two of our boxes bracketing the main target, one hitting the aeroradio station at the Brest Naval School.

* * *

With the Seine in sight, our objective is only a few minutes away. Black flak blossoms among the low and lead boxes, less of it reaching the high where we fly. Our bombs float silently away. Soon the road intersection below erupts into billows of pulverized earth. A quick turn to the left takes us out of the barrage. We angle to the left again, now heading northwest toward the coast and the safety of the English Channel.

I think about the differences between being an airman and being a ground soldier. After a raid, if I make it back, I can sleep in a clean bed in a reasonably comfortable barracks in safe surroundings. He may have to doze in a muddy trench or a cold foxhole, never knowing when the enemy might surprise him. I can walk into a sparkling mess hall where cooks serve hot, appetizing meals while the infantryman may have to rip open a box of K-rations or line up at a hastily erected field kitchen where harried cooks plop "something" into his mess kit.

On the other hand, we expose ourselves to enemy fire without being able to dive into a trench or duck behind thick armor plate. We hang out our lives in fragile, gasoline-laden aluminum cocoons vulnerable to flying shrapnel, all of us riding potential fireballs. We work in an atmosphere of sub-freezing temperatures and air so thin it would kill us if we were not tethered to an oxygen system.

An airman falls a long way when his plane is disabled. If he can get out, he must jump into hostile rarified air, hoping he'll be conscious when he pulls the ring on his parachute. If he survives, the German authorities trundle him off to a stalag.

A flyer's life can be snuffed out as quickly as an infantryman's. The two may perish in different ways, but the dying is the same, and their loved ones grieve for them in the same way.

The men on the ground, especially those in the front lines, see the enemy—real human beings with real faces—whereas I, from five miles up, see no one on the ground. They hear the far off shouts of the enemy, the crack of rifles and the staccato of machine guns. I hear only the hypnotic drone of our own engines. For me it's an almost impersonal war except for what I can imagine.

I know, however, that with the tons of explosives that my fellow bombardiers and I drop, some of them missing their intended targets, that there are surely civilian casualties below. I try to imagine that most of the people huddle in air raid shelters with impenetrable concrete walls. Worried that German gunners are zeroing in on me with their 88 mm artillery, I have little time to think about what people suffer on the ground. Perhaps one of the bombs that I had armed with my own fingers, has leveled a house or destroyed a family, but from 25,000 feet up, I'll never know. My conscience and I bomb factories, airports and rail yards, not people.

By the time we reach Beachy Head across the channel, we've descended to 11,000 feet. We skirt around the west side of London, fluttering through scattered cumulus clouds as we let down toward Polebrook. I think we've aided the Allied troops today, the plastering of the intersection perhaps slowing down the rush of German troops and supplies to the front.

Eleven of our planes had been damaged by flak today, but we all return.

THE MAN WHO LOVED WOMEN

Bill's dominating interest, other than being a good friend to his fellow officers, is women. They people his mind, cavort through his fantasies, flow out on his words. His fingertips itch for them. He inhales their fragrance, tastes them on his lips.

With an impish grin he shows me a photograph of one of his English girlfriends. At first thinking it will be a portrait, I'm amazed that it's a revealing picture of her sitting down in the woods, smiling, her short skirt drawn up to her knees, exposing the very center of her womanhood. "Wow," I say, not being able to think of anything else.

Bill is an enigma to me. I don't approve of his womanizing, yet he is the friendliest bombardier I know. Always smiling slyly, he spreads cheer everywhere whether it's in the mess hall or on the flight line. Even after harrowing raids he keeps his composure, always exuding confidence and optimism as he struts through the barracks talking to his friends. He's no glad-hander or back-slapper, just genuinely eye-contact friendly. He appears to shrug off his missions, acting as though they had never occurred, never letting them distort his outlook on life.

He accepts everyone, no matter how much they differ from him, and, in turn, he expects others to accept him. The only men he has no tolerance for are slackers who fail to perform their duty.

Slender, almost wiry, he walks about briskly with his tempered optimism. He keeps his blondish hair closely cropped, in a "butch" style and wears glasses with wire rims. Not handsome in the rugged male sense, he is most good looking when he smiles, revealing his even white teeth. He strides and stands as erectly as a career officer.

Bill tells us he has a whole gallery of photographs on the wall around his bunk. When he lies on his bed, his women in various degrees of undress surround him. "Come on over," he says, "I'll show them to you." The rest follow him over to his barracks, but I decide not to go with them. "I don't think I'll go, Bill," I say. He answers with his usual warmth, "Okay. I'll see you later."

Even though I pass up his offer, he greets me with his same enveloping friendliness the next time he sees me. Instead of teasing me or making smart remarks about my "purity" or "innocence" or "prudishness," he respects my point of view. I, in turn, respect him for this uncommon attitude. I still accept him as a person despite my not approving of his morals.

Bill finds women everywhere, even on the base. He and a woman are like two drops of water that by simply brushing each other, instantly merge and coalesce into one.

"I was riding my bicycle through the woods toward the base theater the other day when I saw a woman sitting near the path," says Bill. "I stopped my bike and talked to her for a while. She agreed to go back into the woods with me." He beams when he tells me this story about his "unusual opportunity."

Bill is married and writes home frequently to his wife, yet his life seems to be devoted to the pursuit of females. I can't understand how a man who loves his wife and professes to have a high regard for her can seek out other women. Does his wife know what he does? Does she accept it? Does he feel no guilt? Does he genuinely love his wife, yet feel that he has his "rights" as a man with an intense sexual appetite? How does he keep love and sex apart in his mind?

I personally believe that sex and love should be melded, each of the two passions enhancing the other, in a marriage to one woman to whom one is faithful. Bill's outlook is exactly opposite.

Bill had been a Flight Officer when he was first commissioned, wearing blue and gold bars rounded at the ends. He had quickly been promoted to Second Lieutenant, and today to First Lieutenant. To help him celebrate, he invites some of us to go with him to the Church Army building, a service run on the base by the Church of England, where he'll treat us to tea and sandwiches.

The weather had turned cold. Forcing ourselves out of bed in the chilly barracks had been very difficult, almost painful. The warmth of the Church Army room feels pleasant, and the babble of our voices as we sip steaming tea and nibble tiny English sandwiches, adds to the coziness.

"Well, how does it feel to be a first lieutenant, Bill?"

"Damn good. I didn't think they'd ever give it to me since I came in here as an FO."

"You deserve it. How many missions do you have now?"

179

"I don't know exactly, but it's getting close to thirty."

"Pass me another sandwich, will ya? They're itsy-bitsy things, but they sure taste good."

"Anyone for more tea?"

I can't help but think of the irony of Bill, the adulterer, celebrating his promotion in a place sponsored by the church. But we all like him, and he likes us, and this is wartime, and we are all by random coincidence here together, savoring one of our few good times.

SCHKEUDITZ AND THOUGHTS ABOUT HOME

After three raids into France in support of our ground troops, we're on a mission deep into Germany again, our planes' bellies pregnant with 500-pound incendiary clusters, enough to incinerate the aircraft factory at Schkeuditz near Leipzig. We've just crossed the Dutch coast, heading east into the sun. Amsterdam lies thirty miles south of us. It is 0900. The aircraft factory is still two and one-half hours away.

Silver fleets of bombers stretch out ahead of us, the sun glinting off their wings and tails like sparkles from the facets of jewels. Squadrons of American fighter planes patrol the skies above us. Luftwaffe pilots rarely attack when we're protected, but they always know where we are. They wait patiently for their opportunities.

Soon passing into Germany, I look ahead through my great Plexiglas "bay window," watching nearby formations and for any sign of the enemy. Only a slight haze dims the land below. It is a rare clear day for looking down at the fields, farmhouses and villages, the rivers and forests of our adversary. From my bombardier's seat at 25,000 feet Germany appears to be a country of magnificent scenery and clean, tidy towns. I find it odd that our enemy lives in such attractive surroundings. Why can't they be satisfied with all that beauty instead of forcing death and destruction on the other people of Europe? I often wonder what they do down there in the open country, hearing the approach of our thunder. Do they run for shelter, or do they just go about plowing their fields and cutting hay?

I've been stationed in England over three months now, and I ache with homesickness. My feelings are an amalgam of wanting to be safe and away from the tension of the war and yearning for the love and comfort of the hearth.

I had felt uncomfortable about being in Scotland during my mother's and sister's birthdays which are on the same day, because I wouldn't be able to write them. I'd written them later about making it all up when I return. I wanted them to have a happy birthday and hoped I would be with them the next time those special days rolled around.

We veer off toward the southeast so that we can later loop back toward the target. We still have one and one-half hours of flying time before we arrive. The briefing officers warned us that the German air defenses would be substantial, but I try not to think about it. Along the way several antiaircraft batteries had taken pot shots at our formations, but most bursts were far off the mark.

I'd written home two days before without very much to say because I couldn't write a word about our military operation. I again expressed my homesickness, how much I wanted to be home by Christmas, how ecstatic I'd be when I got home.

My sister, Charline, is about to leave home for nurse cadet training. I couldn't resist giving her brotherly advice. I told her how sorry I had been to leave home, but that I was anxious to get started on what I was going to do. I warned her that taking orders and being "racked back" were hard to live with but to not take them personally. I let her know that she would run up against rules, regulations and orders that seem crazy or silly, but she must abide by them anyway. Lastly I noted that she would meet all kinds of people with varying personalities. Some might shock her at first. I advised her to be always friendly, but not to follow in their footsteps, to live the way she was brought up to live.

Nearing the aircraft plant, the Siebel Flugzeug Werke, I forget about home, all thoughts of family and friends evaporating. I become engrossed in what I have to do, the apprehension of what lies ahead. We approach in a large fishhook pattern, flying southeast at first then swinging around to the left until we come upon the target from the northeast. As usual with objectives over Germany, the coalesced bursts of hundreds of antiaircraft rounds smudge the place where we must fly, an ugly smear in the pristine air. They can see us clearly today. They'll be tracking us.

All during the bomb run the Nazi gunners pummel us with flak, following us well, their shells bursting among us like vicious shaggy black dogs, nipping and snarling. One of our planes loses two engines, begins to drop in altitude as it falls behind. Its chances of making it back are slim.

Our incendiary clusters fall quietly away, 120 of them all at once, crowding the sky, all aimed toward the aircraft plant. We turn sharply to the right. Explosions smother the hangers and shops below. The high and low boxes hit the target also, but nearly create a catastrophe of their own making when the low box inadvertently slides under the high on the bomb run, some of their loads barely missing the planes below. We'd heard stories about higher groups endangering other planes below them. In one account a bomb had ripped through the astrodome of one B-17, instantly killing the navigator.

Tattered and frayed by shrapnel, we turn towards the west and "home." Lieutenant Cartwright's plane is now out of sight and presumably lost. Parts of the Leipzig outer defenses pick us up, harassing us with more flak on the way out. At Halle they shoot at us again.

I'm more homesick than ever on our way back to England. This has been our 24th mission. I have somehow gotten away with it 24 times and hope that my luck will last. Lieutenant Cartwright's crew didn't get away with it today.

My parents had written me that they might make some changes in my room in the garage at home. I urgently requested that they not change anything, especially my bed, a place I would like to be right now, peaceful and dark with the rhythmic sounds of crickets outside my window, the faint smell of wallboard, a barely visible photograph of Veronica Lake with her long blond hair curved in toward one eye.

TWO FRIENDS

As I walk along the asphalt road near our barracks, I approach a small group of men coming toward me. They chat excitedly with each other while they stroll in a close but awkward knot. They appear to be unsure about where they're going. Perhaps they're a new crew. Out of curiosity, I look at them when we pass. Instantly I recognize one of those faces.

"Ballantyne," I shout, turning my head back to them.

"Hi, Stevens", he says, "are you at this base too?"

"Yeah," I reply, "I've been here for quite a while. I'm sure glad to see you again. What squadron have you been assigned to?"

As we shake hands, he says, "The 509th. Which one are you in?"

Still grasping his hand, I reply, "The same one. So I guess we'll be flying together."

At his crew's urging he begins to drift away with them, shouting back to me, "Nice seeing you again, Stevens. I'll catch you later."

I hadn't seen Glenn Ballantyne in months, not since we'd left snowy Salt Lake City in January. He'd been assigned to the Midwest, Sioux City, Iowa, for his crew training while I went to the South, to Alexandria, Louisiana.

I'm pleased that such a former fast friend has ended up on the same combat base with me. The idea of our flying together is somehow comforting. We'd shared a barracks room all through bombardier training at Midland, Texas where our friendship had grown. I admired his quiet seriousness, his drive to study, his goal to make it through training. He was the first person I had ever met who genuinely loved knowledge and studying, and was not afraid to say so.

"You know, Stevens, I just love to hit the books. I really look forward to college after the war, probably at the University of Washington or possibly Washington State. I can hardly wait."

I also liked his friendliness, gentleness and determination. He had character. He was a genuine human being.

Although my ambition to win my bombardier's wings matched his, his daily example of studying hard and liking it, being proud of it even, encouraged me to do the same. His desire to attend college after the war also influenced my decision to consider going to UCLA.

Pushing through my barracks door, I think about being reunited with Ballantyne. It's almost like seeing a member of my family again. He still looks the same, his droopy hat cockeyed on his head, his uniform wrinkled, his shoulders slightly hunched. He'd never been a ramrod like some super cadets or neat and tidy with his clothes. None of this mattered to him. He dressed just well enough and stood just straight enough to escape criticism.

I see little of him in the days that follow. He and his crew were assigned to another barracks, and he had formed a solid camaraderie with his crew, just as I had with mine. We were also busy flying missions and sleeping off fatigue, giving us little time to be together.

On a mission to Central Germany, I recognize Ballantyne's plane in our formation, off to our left. I can almost wave to him. Our bombers drone along together, the sun highlighting their bright, unpainted skins.

After dropping our bombs and flying through the usual flak barrage, I look over to see Ballantyne's plane on fire, orange flames flowing back from its two right engines, licking around the wing. Dumbfounded I stare at it, hoping it won't blow up, holding my breath, horrified. Suddenly the plane breaks formation. It dives straight down, bright flames trailing it like the blaze of a falling torch. Down it plummets, almost out of sight now in the haze, still on fire. Then I don't see it any more.

"Bombardier to pilot."

Two clicks on the intercom.

"Did you see that? He dove straight down. What do you think happened?"

"I think he did it to put out the fire. He might have been able to do it."

My throat tightens. I run the vision of the plunging bomber through my mind, over and over. Even if the pilot managed to snuff out the fire, what chance would he have now, alone over Germany with hungry predators on the lookout for the weak, injured and alone? The fighters will find them. I'm sure of it.

Several days later, I hear from headquarters that he and other members of his crew are prisoners of war.   Apparently enemy interceptors had picked them off, but at least some of them had parachuted to safety.

I'm glad to know that Ballantyne is alive, but I mourn his not being with us any more.   It is August 1944, and the American Army has reached Paris.   The ground war is going well, but how many months lie ahead?   How long will he have to endure a German Stalag?   I want him to attend the University of Washington.

* * *

I don't make friends easily.   Even though I'm friendly to almost all the men, I'm only close to a very few.   I realize I'm different from most.   I don't have that aggressive, egocentric slouch that some have— that hard-hearted toughness, obstinate impatience and insensitivity, that casual lack of inhibitions that characterize some.   I get along with men like that, but when I'm on my own time, I choose not to pal around with them.   I don't consider myself better or worse than they are, only different.

I'd become acquainted with the navigator of one of the crews in the next barracks.   About my height, he combed his wavy blondish hair straight back, the small waves in front growing larger as they rippled in regular rhythm toward the back of his head. A gentle smile lit up his fair complexion, his prominent nose thrust forward.

I'd liked communicating with another man without reservation, without steering through verbal garbage, without speaking self-consciously or running an obstacle course of words. To him I had been able to converse cleanly, crisply and directly. He'd often gone to the movies with us or accompanied us to the mess hall. We enjoyed talking about the same topics—our families back home, our flying experiences, even the weather.

On our raid to Augsburg, Focke-Wulf 190s had sent his plane down, spinning, on fire and out of control. I thought to myself how odd it was. When men became my good friends, they were shot down. The navigator had been such a nice man, but Focke-Wulf 190s and flak kill princes and bastards impartially.

We never hear any more about the crew, never knowing whether they were able to leap free to become prisoners or whether they had perished.

I think more about why good men die and others that I consider not so good return from raids again and again. Why had God allowed this to happen? The question weighs heavily on me during our missions. I pray to God to protect me, to watch over me, but I begin to wonder why I should expect Him to take any special interest in me or any particular person, whether He really shelters anyone.

THE BRIDGE AT NAMUR

By the time we turn south over the outer Dutch islands, our three squadrons have already reached 25,000 feet. I've never flown a mission this late in the day. The low angle of the sun, the eerie light and shadows on the clouds and ground present a sense of unreality, as though we're not supposed to be there. Our wheels had left the Polebrook runway at 1630 hours.

I'm troubled about our target, the railroad bridge across the Meuse at Namur, Belgium, because clusters of buildings are at each end of it, probably apartments, shops and business offices, the city being built right up to it. Large cumulus clouds wallow across the land, and even though we can see the ground below through breaks between them, they pose potential problems in sighting on the span. It's very important that we knock it out as it's on a major supply line to bolster the German troops pouring into the front. We fly at the tail end of the low box, a bad position for flak if the target is well defended.

Our group continues flying south, passing far to the west of Antwerp with its bristling flak batteries. Shortly after 1800 hours we change course toward the northeast and the vital link at Namur. Mounds of clouds still obscure much of the ground, but clear spaces between them allow us to make out pieces of roads, villages and rivers. As we close in on the city, the bridge appears ahead of us in a large break. All the bombardiers slowly open their bomb bay doors.

Antiaircraft fire begins to explode around us. The gunners are accurate, but there aren't many of them.

At the end of our run, at the last few seconds, a large cloud slides over the bridge. We salvo our bombs anyway, our box alone releasing seventy-two 1000-pound bombs, the massive load sinking silently down toward the mist. I can only hope that the lead bombardier had been accurate, that the last minute interference had not spoiled his aim. More undercast hides the impact of our bombs. We don't know whether we twisted the steel girders of the bridge, churned up the Meuse River or, worse yet, turned a section of town into rubble.

On our way back to the Dutch islands, I hope for the best, but I'm concerned about having hit the city. I'd not been responsible for aiming our bombs, but I'd let mine go when the lead bombardier released his, our normal procedure. My missiles are among the swarm that had streaked toward whatever they hit. I think about it on the way back to England.

We let down through thick broken clouds over England, arriving at Polebrook near 2000 hours.

We find out that the lead bombardier, having zeroed in on the bridge, the bombsight's crosshairs sticking right on it, had let his bombs go even though the cloud had obscured his vision at the very end. Since he'd been so well synchronized, he decided to let his bombs go anyway. He didn't want to make another run on the target for fear of interfering with our other two boxes and the following groups. He doesn't know what he hit.

I think about it at night, that we might have killed some innocent people, Belgian's, our friends. Not until the next day do we find out exactly what our results were. Our other two boxes had bracketed the bridge, but our bombs had sailed straight into the south side of the city, almost a half-mile short of the bridge. Had the lead bombardier been able to see the target, he would have detected the range hair of his bombsight creeping back almost imperceptibly. A minor correction would have put the bombs where they belonged, but he had to make a split-second decision then abide by it.

I feel uneasy about having hit the town, and I'm sorry for the people. I hope they'd been safely tucked away in air raid shelters. Fantasies of death and destruction float through my mind, apartments and shops erupting into smoke and jagged stones. It's all part of the insanity of war, friends and enemies, the innocent and guilty suffering alike.

Rain drips from the barracks roof, and the cold gloom of the day presses against the windows as I try to write a short letter home. I can't tell them anything about what happened or what I'm feeling. The Belgian town is still on my mind, but I try to push it to the far edges of my consciousness.

I turn my thoughts to home, answering the questions my parents had asked in their last letter. I tell them why I couldn't write yesterday—"due to obvious reasons"—, and I tell them about the rain. They had written that Louis, a relative in the Air Corps, had been shot down in the Pacific, and that they believed that it was unjust to send him against a target where the odds were so much against them. I respond with:

"But that is the way war goes. Just or unjust, if a target must be bombed, it will be bombed, and that's all there is to it."

They remind me once more about making some changes in my room at home, my place in the garage that I constantly think about. For some reason I can't bear to imagine it's being any different than it was the day I left. I write:

"No. I don't want my room out there papered. I like it just the way it is. Don't ever change my mattress either. I like that one. As hard as it is, it's much more soft and comfortable than what I sleep on now. I was really sore the first few nights I slept on it."

Thinking about home helps, but the nagging specter of what happened at Namur will be with me for a while.

CHARLES N. STEVENS

LONDON—ONE MORE TIME

"We were hit by a buzz bomb yesterday, so things are somewhat chaotic today," explains the desk clerk at the Mayfair. "The only room we can offer you is one on the ground floor that was partially damaged in the explosion. It will have no door, and the glass is out of at least one of the windows, but it's clean, and the bed will be comfortable."

Having nowhere else to go, and not having anything valuable with us except our own lives, Podoske and I accept the quarters.

After having some close calls with buzz bombs on the two previous trips, we'd vowed never to return to London until the rain of these missiles had stopped. At that time, however, we didn't know that we'd be promoted to First Lieutenants and that London would be the only place where we could buy silver Lieutenants bars. Anxious to display our new rank, our pride and vanity had brought us back. We now outrank all of the crews in our barracks, and we want to revel in our "superiority", flaunt it quietly.

We check out our room that looks just fine except for the blown-off door and the missing glass then head off down the London sidewalks to find the military shop that sells hardware and insignias. A fine drizzle drifts down, prickling our faces, and dampening the streets and sidewalks. Windshield wipers on the taxies and buses sweep back and forth, clearing the mist. The wet streets mirror the low-hanging blanket of clouds, and taxi tires hiss on the pavement.

The cozy warmth of the shop feels good to us as we approach the glass counter where the brass is displayed under a brilliant light. Even before we leave the shop, we attach the silver bars to our shoulders. We begin to feel our rank, puff up a little, walk a bit more gracefully. We're combat veterans now and have the metal to prove it.

Despite the off and on drizzle, we join the civilians and soldiers on the street, sporting our shiny new bars. After several hours, tired of walking and looking, we duck into a theater to see a movie called "Once Upon a Time" with Cary Grant, Janet Blair and James Gleason. It's about a slightly crooked showman down on his luck that discovers a boy who has a dancing caterpillar. He charges people to see it dance. The strange film takes us away from the war, transports us to a totally different world.

The misting had stopped when we emerge from the theater, but the mournful air raid sirens sound once again as they had earlier in the day, when we had listened to the terrifying sound of the buzz bombs as they rumbled and putted over London. We heard the faraway thud of their impacts several times. We'd asked ourselves again whether returning to London to buy our silver bars had been worth it.

In the evening Podoske and I join Warren and Johnston for dinner in the Mayfair dining room. We sit in fancy cream-colored chairs around a white-clothed table, enjoying the luxury of the room's elegant ambience and the attentive service. The rest of them have drinks, but I decline as I still, even after 25 harrowing missions, stubbornly feel the same way about alcohol. I don't make the mistake of ordering cider, now that I know what it really is. My crew tolerates me, respecting my feelings about drinking. I, in return, respect them, and never object to their imbibing.

After dinner, I wander back to our doorless room, soon going to bed. Podoske had gone out. More air raid sirens moan in the night, and I hear more V-1s in the distance, their distinctive throbbing, the muffled thumps of their strikes, like a single blow on a base drum. I would think that with all of the bombing raids on their launching sites, and the taking of French territory by the Allied Forces, that the number of attacks would be diminished, but they keep coming, seemingly more than ever.

I think about what an Englishman said to me on the street.

"Well, our troops are taking more and more territory each day in western France. We'll have butter again soon."

He'd irritated me. With all the soldiers being killed and wounded on the front, this guy can only think about having his butter again. His remarks seem selfish and petty to me. Yet, I suppose it was an expression of wanting to return to normalcy after suffering years of deprivation.

The next morning Podoske and I both swear again that we'll never return to London as long as those pesky Nazi weapons continue to pelt it. It's foolish, after risking our skins on our bombing missions, to expose ourselves to their random terror.

We gather our meager belongings, and walk up to the desk to check out. The clerk calculates our bill, then looks up, and says, "Your key sir?"

I smile, and say, "We didn't have any door on our room, so they didn't give us a key."

He chuckles, and says, "Okay, I forgot about that."

THE ARMAMENT WORKS AT WEIMAR

Flying over the North Sea is like drifting over a blue featureless wasteland. I can't follow a map as I usually do over land when it's clear, so there's little for me to do but think. I've checked my guns, pulled the pins on the bombs and reviewed my intervalometer settings, but we still have two hours of flying time left over the sea before we turn inland. I keep my eyes open for possible fighter attacks, but the chances of encountering them out here, especially with squadrons of American P-47 fighters sticking close to us, is quite remote.

Our engines labor as we climb from 6500 feet to our assigned altitude of 25,000 feet that we must reach by the time we arrive at the German coastline. Because of thick clouds in England, we'd had to assemble beneath them and then leave flying lower than normal.

A hazy nothingness lies before me, marked only with the dim formations of the bombers ahead. They still remind me of orderly flocks of geese flying south for the winter. Warren keeps track of our position on his G-Box, checking the little quivering green blips on his oscilloscope. Johnston is about the only person working as he adjusts the throttles, rudder and elevators to keep us in a tight formation. Lucas, the engineer, watches the gauges, and Witherspoon with his earphones monitors the radio. The gunners wait.

Even though the North Sea is murky, my mind isn't. Behind my oxygen mask and cupped in my leather flying helmet with its earphones, my mind entertains a myriad of thoughts and fantasies, most of them centering on the apprehension of the mission ahead. I answer my own questions about the possible flak, the, likelihood of being suddenly jumped by bandits, whether my bombs will release properly. My brain supplies me with quiet motion pictures about each event, the movies sometimes contradicting each other.

Tired of the futility of outguessing the eventual reality of the mission, I think about home, as I always do. My parents had written me about the newspapers at home carrying a story concerning American bombers that had pummeled our own troops. I told them that it was another group that had bombed short of the target, that I hadn't been involved.

They also wrote me about people going on strike at home, and refusing to work unless their pay was raised. The news infuriated me. Those workers were making more money than they ever had and living in perfect safety. They could go home every night for a nice meal and read the newspaper in the comfort of their easy chairs. What could be more ideal?

Just before 1100 hours we cross the north coast into Germany. Our route takes us southeast, midway between the heavily defended centers of Bremen and Hamburg on a path headed almost directly towards Berlin. It's obvious that the route was designed to shake up the defensive forces at these large cities even though we hadn't planned to bomb any of them, our target being at Weimar, a considerable distance southwest of Berlin. Our mission planners had hoped that by flying close to these places, we'd stir up their fighters so that ours could knock them down. It's a little like throwing a stone at a hornet's nest then picking off the bees as they swarm out. Our problem is that the enraged insects may choose to sting us before our fighters swat them down.

At first all is well. We see no enemy aircraft, and the little flak we encounter is futile and inaccurate.

"Pilot to crew. They're reporting plenty of interceptors in the area so be alert."

As we pass by Berlin on the west side, bandits attack the group behind us, sending several of their ships down. Johnston says they report being assaulted by Focke-Wulf 190s, Messerschmitt 109s, Junkers 88s and Messerschmitt 410s, almost every type of airplane in their arsenal. The tail gunner shouts over the intercom.

"They hit the group behind us! Some of the bandits are swinging underneath us!"

I look down through my Plexiglas window as ten or twelve Messerschmitt 109s streak beneath us flying in close formation, concentrating their firepower. Just out of range, the sleek gunmetal-gray fighters with German crosses on their wings ignore us, choosing instead to swoop up to the tail end of the group in front of us. Almost immediately one of their B-17s explodes.

Somehow, at least for now, the spin of the roulette wheel has once more been in our favor. Once again we get away with it, all of the action happening so fast that I hardly have time to react. Maybe our tight formation looked too formidable to them, or maybe we were simply not in their plan. As we fly into the area of the attack a parachute floats down, its silk a mottled tan, almost tobacco brown, the tiny silhouette of a man dangling from the shroud lines. He must be a German fighter pilot, probably from one of those Messerschmitts shot down in the attack on the bombers, I say to myself. As we pass by the descending parachute, I look again at the diminutive body of the man, the space between his legs barely visible. If he's a German pilot, he's the first German I've ever seen, the war up until now being entirely impersonal, the people on the ground invisible from 25,000 feet. He intrigues me. I begin to wonder about his name, his face, how he feels settling slowly down to earth, how cold he must be.

We quickly leave the parachuter behind, turning sharply to direct south so that we can approach the armament works from the east. The bandits have fled, undoubtedly chased by our own P-51 Mustang fighters. We begin the bomb run, our bomb bays open, ready to release our 500-pounders. Flak in the target area is sporadic and off the mark, unusual for any target in German territory. Groups ahead have already struck the armament works, smoke and fire boiling out of the sprawling buildings. Our bombs strike structures that haven't yet been hit.

Our work done, we lumber back toward the north coast, still an hour away, and all of it over Germany. We avoid areas of heavy flak concentrations, but still must watch for fighters near Hanover and Bremen. All is clear. By 1330 hours in the afternoon we pass over the coastline and the relative safety of the North Sea and the English Channel beyond. I feel my muscles relax. The tightness in my shoulders, back and butt loosen. I bask in the usual levity of returning safely. Whoever is or is not responsible—God, chance, fate, circumstance, and luck—has or has not pulled me through again.

We roar back over England, beneath a ragged gray sky, occasional showers streaming against my Plexiglas window, the quivering drops creeping over the glass in all directions. By 1530 hours we settle into the wet runways at Polebrook.

IN CASE WE GO DOWN

Light from the screen flickers on the faces of the crews gathered in the assembly room for another training film. Pictured is a German officer kindly offering a cigarette to an American airman brought into his office from a downed bomber. Treating him with respect, the interrogator smiles pleasantly as he routinely asks him his name, rank and serial number.

"John R. Thompson, First Lieutenant, 0704242," replies the uneasy prisoner.

In the same friendly manner, the German in his high-peaked cap and immaculate uniform asks, "What is the number of your bomb group? What is the name of your base?"

The American, obviously uncomfortable, says," I can't tell you that, sir."

The questioner, never losing his smile or composure, says, "We have ways of finding out anyway, but it is easier for you simply to tell us." The captive still refuses to answer the question. According to the rules of the Geneva Convention, prisoners of war are only required to supply the information he had already provided.

"Oh, by the way, I have a surprise for you," he says. "The pilot who shot your plane down yesterday is here and wants to meet you. You know, it was a special day for him; it was his birthday."

The tactic takes advantage of the American fondness for sentimentality.

A Nazi intelligence officer, wearing the uniform of a German Luftwaffe pilot, wings shining on his tunic, steps into the room, his hand extended to the American officer. They shake hands.

"I hope there are no hard feelings. It was simply my duty to shoot down American bombers. And, as he has probably told you, it was my special day yesterday. Even though we are fighting on different sides, we are all part of the brotherhood of airmen. There should be no barriers between us—we can talk like brothers."

The film warns us of the ploy and cautions us that if shot down and captured we should be aware of their strategies.

It also informs us that they might use force as a tactic to help them gain information, such as threatening us with punishment or slapping us around. Still, we are to give them only our name, rank and serial number. Severe beatings or torture are against the Geneva rulings and probably are not to be feared.

We often talk among ourselves about what we might expect if we should have to bail out over Germany. We hear many stories about what happens to airmen if civilians catch them. We've heard tales about farmers with pitchforks who would like to make shish kabob out of us, or mobs who would beat us to death. In the event that we have to bail out, we hope that we escape from everyone or at least are picked up by the police or military authorities that would transfer us to a stalag. The German people naturally hate us for destroying their industry and cities, and especially for causing civilian casualties, perhaps some of them family members, relatives or friends. With the help of a propaganda machine that labels us as killers of women and children, the German people consider us all devils and monsters, fit to be exterminated if we should fall in their midst. I carry my .45 pistol with me on my missions, mainly to protect myself from civilians. I practice with it on the base range, but I never become an expert marksman, having a tendency to shoot far below where I aim. At least I might be able to frighten people with it, ward them off until the authorities arrive.

Leaping from a bomber at 25,000 feet is an ordeal in itself. Once an airman is free of his plane, he must face freezing temperatures and an acute lack of oxygen. The recommended procedure is to attach a bail-out bottle, a small container of compressed oxygen, to the mask, then delay the opening of the parachute so that the fast fall quickly takes him down to a lower, safer altitude. Most men I have seen jump open theirs immediately, the most natural reaction when they find themselves hurtling through the air five miles above the ground. They float away from the disabled plane like feathered fluff blown from a dandelion head. If the bomber blows up, and the crewman survives, his only hope is that his parachute is still attached and that it is undamaged. They must jump quickly when the pilot sounds the alarm, since hesitation may worsen their chances of getting out of a plane that later lurches out of control, spins or tumbles, catches fire or explodes.

My escape hatch is small, a door in the bottom of the fuselage just past the navigator's compartment. I often wonder about facing the rush of air pouring through the opening, squeezing through it with my flying clothes and the bulkiness of my chest chute. I'm supposed to place my feet on the edge then tumble through, head first. I had never done this during training, had never wanted to. We practice landings by jumping off of a 6-foot platform into a sawdust pit. They teach us to land with our feet together, our knees slightly bent, then to roll when we hit, breaking the impact of our fall.

Our instructors advise us to bury our equipment, then run away from the place where we land. If we settle into Holland or France there is the chance that members of the underground will pick us up, then help us to hide or escape. They even tell us how to act French by letting our cigarettes dangle from our lips. If an airman smokes a cigarette like an American, he is easily detected.

Many crippled bombers had been able to limp out of Germany, only to find that they couldn't make it across the channel. The crew's sole recourse is to bail out over the water and take their chances of being rescued, or ditch the plane. To accomplish this maneuver the pilot has to belly-land on the water, dragging the tail at first to slow it then easing the nose down. Crewmen have to brace themselves for the impact then scramble out of escape hatches on top, remembering not to inflate their life jackets until they are clear. They then deploy dinghies, entering them carefully from on top of the wings. Once in, the crew must paddle away from the plane, but not too far, as the plane itself, or at least its oil slick, will be visible to rescue crews who search the area. All of us practice ditching drills on the base in an old B-17 without landing gear, first assuming our braced positions, then hustling out through the top to walk along the wings. Ditching is always dangerous. The airplane might not withstand the impact, or crewmembers might not survive the shock. They also risk not being found by the air-sea rescue service. We all hope we never have to land in the water, but many do. The floor of the channel must be littered with old B-17s and B-24s.

Every day, bomber crews, sometimes many of them, have to abandon their planes. Even though I'm aware of the grim possibilities, the sting of it is countered by the naive belief that it will always happen to somebody else. It's a peculiar egocentric belief that "protects" me from the reality of statistics. I have a bad case of this concept and a related conviction that everything will always be okay, always believing that my bombs will drop correctly, that my guns will fire accurately if I need them, that the flak will not hit our plane, that we will never have to bail out or ditch. Everything will be okay.

CHARLES N. STEVENS

AN AFTERNOON MILK RUN

Stuffing the two letters in my flying suit, I hurry down to the briefing room. Mail from home just before the mission eases my apprehensions. The late afternoon assignment surprises us. We'd looked forward to a day of rest and leisure after most of the crews had gone for a morning assault on the rocket experimental facilities at Peenemunde, Germany.

Taking off shortly after 1600 hours, twelve planes from our field join small forces from other bases for an attack on an oxygen plant at Henin-Lietard, France, north of Paris. Just before leaving the English coast at Selsey Bill, I pull the pins on my 500-pound bombs.

Returning to the bombardier's compartment, I fish out the letters—still plenty of time to read them before we reach the French coast. As we climb steadily over the channel, I open the one from home first. My mind quickly turns away from our military business toward Inglewood thousands of miles away, almost quieting the low throb of our engines. I hold the letter in my glove, peering out over the top of my oxygen mask at my mother's familiar handwriting.

Several small samples of wallpaper fall out of the envelope, clipped scraps from what they'd been hanging in several rooms of the house. I hold the bits in my glove, trying to imagine how the newly decorated wall would look. I think the design is attractive, that they had made a wise choice. The job had cost them seventy dollars. Worrying about the expense, I plan to offer them some of my savings.

Now that I've saved so much money, I want to help them out. Contributing makes me feel more like an adult.

My sister, Charline, has left home for nurse cadet training, and I'm concerned that my mother and father will be lonely. I vow to write more often, even if I'm dead tired. I can at least dash off a note to them each day. For nineteen years my sister and I had been a vital part of their lives, but now the house is quiet and, I think, empty for them. They still work long hours in the garage silver-soldering brass fittings onto flexible metal hoses for aircraft engines, but the house, especially the kitchen and dining nook, must seem quite barren.

They write that one of Charline's friends had entered the training program with her. I feel good about that. Having someone with her for companionship will make life away from home easier. I know how much smoother my beginnings in the army at Fort MacArthur had been with Howard Berry, Don Olson and Bill Hoy there, all from my class at Inglewood High School. I often think about them. Howard Berry and Bill Hoy are now both pilots, I am a bombardier and Don is a gunner on a B-24, training at Muroc, California. I miss seeing them now.

My parents ask me, for some reason, whether I'll act differently after I get home, fearing, I suppose, that army life and particularly combat might have altered my personality. I think it's a good question, but I don't know how I would really know if I'd changed. Only they will be able to detect it when they see me again. Experiences, especially emotional ones, do change people, but I believe my outlook on life, my moral and spiritual beliefs are all still intact.

I breeze over a very light letter from my "girlfriend" then bring my mind back to the present, the French coast looming up before us. We pass over it midway between Le Havre and Cherbourg, at first angling toward the southeast. We shortly turn abruptly to the left on a line directed right at Paris. Before reaching it, we bank to the left on a more northerly course.

On the final run, our bomb bay doors open, we see no flak at all. I expect it to begin bursting at any moment, but the sky remains clear, a complete surprise. I watch the lead ship, ready to salvo my 500-pounders. As the lead bombardier's load floats out of his plane's belly, I flip my salvo switch, but nothing happens. I quickly check my indicator lights. Everything seems okay, but the reluctant bombs will not release. We're going to have to take them back. Having had two failed drops blamed on me back in July, I worry that this is a return to my bad luck.

Back over the channel, I slip in the cotter pins again, disarming the bombs. The flight had been easy, a short one with no opposition—a milk-run. We need opportunities like this periodically to bolster our morale. It counts on our tally as much as one to a well-defended target in Germany.

The mechanics find that the fuse to the salvo circuit had burned out, preventing me from dropping the bombs, a great relief to me.

Again chance had played its part on August 25, 1944. The majority of our crews had endured a long mission to Peenemunde, Germany where they'd encountered the usual heavy flak barrages, damaging ten of our planes, seven of them severely. We had breezed through a short mission with no flak at all— another roll of the dice.

THE POLEBROOK MENAGERIE

Perched on my shoulder, the little monkey searches my shirt pocket. Finding nothing, he jumps down beside me, rifles through my jacket where he discovers a stick of gum. He quickly runs away with it. I don't know who actually owns the animal or where he had come from, but he feels right at home among us, making the rounds of the barracks, usually with one of the men. The smart little scamp knows exactly what he wants and where he can find it. He first leaps to our shoulders then deftly leans over to search our shirt pockets, throwing away any item he doesn't want. His aim is to find gum. If he finds it, he sits on our shoulders or arms and unwraps the stick, tossing the wrappers on the floor. He pops the sweet stuff in his mouth and chews it.

Even though the monkey is pesky, we enjoy having him on the base. His clown-like antics and his human-like capers help divert us from our grim business. He gives us something to laugh about.

Dogs also wandered on the base looking for human companionship and a bite to eat. One strayed into our barracks, liked us, and decided to stay. He padded around among our beds during the day and slept with us at night. Several days later he left, undoubtedly finding another barracks more to his liking. We liked having him with us. He added a kind of hominess to our lives. I also missed my dog, Pal, at home, the barracks mongrel acting as his surrogate.

Another dog once stayed with us for several days. Smarter than the other one, he pulled an army blanket off an officer's bed with his teeth then used it to sleep on during the night.

Other Fidos often strolled into the Officer's Club. I wrote home about them. "They just drop in as though they are officers, mosey around, 'talk' with the men, sleep a while, and then leave." No one tried to shoo them out because we all wanted them around, their presence providing a nice domestic touch.

I also wrote about cats. "We have a little kitten over in the Officer's Club now. I never saw a cat sleep so much in all my life. Every time I see him he's curled up somewhere. He sleeps in all positions anywhere he chooses, often with the soft fur of his belly arched up." In a way, the softness of the cat contrasts sharply with the harshness of combat flying. No one ever disturbs it from its perpetual slumber. I envy the cat. We're often up early, exhausted from flying and from the tensions of our missions. The cat, on the other hand, has a safe little life and sleeps his fill every day.

One day a small yellow kitten found its way into our barracks. I picked it up, placing it on my bed. It felt so soft and warm in my hands, its tiny body vibrating with its purring. It stayed with me all day then slept on my bed at night. Cats often snoozed at the foot of my bed at home, and this small yellow bundle of fur briefly made me feel as though I was there. The tiny thing disappeared the following day after I returned from a mission, and I sorely missed it.

Somehow a rooster wandered away from one of the surrounding farms, and claimed our part of the base as his territory. He pecked around outside all day then roosted in our latrine out back every night. No one disturbed him as he rested in the shadows.

I like having the animals around. Somehow, whether they remind us of home or simply a normal life, they are comforting.

BIG "B"

A hush falls over the men as the parting curtains reveal our target for today, Berlin or "Big B," as we call it. Out of the quiet several mutter, "Oh, my God," "Jesus Christ" or just plain "Aw shit." The red yarn on the map takes us right over the heart of the city, the armament factory we're to hit unfortunately located in the center of the most heavily defended place in Germany. I feel sure that some of us will not come back. Maybe my luck has run out. I sense that inwardly we are cold and gray about our chances, but outwardly we assume our usual sober stoic stance. There's a job we have to do, and, as always, we'll do it.

I can't help but remember a Hollywood movie I'd seen about the same situation, a briefing where the crews are informed that they will be on a bombing raid to Berlin. Their reaction had been a unanimous loud cheer. They were given the opportunity to fly into the heart of Nazidom and strike a mortal blow at the enemy! Hooray! How phony it all was, how ridiculous! It was a movie made specifically to raise morale at home. How could they have cheered when many of them must have known that they would never return?

With tight lips and an uneasy queasiness in my belly, I listen to the briefing officer. We are to fly out over the North Sea, cross the Danish Peninsula to the Baltic Sea, then turn southeast toward the German mainland. We are to take a course to a point southeast of Berlin, then swing around, and attack the target from the south, not turning sharply to the east until we're directly over the center of the capital. Afterwards we're to flee northward to the Baltic Sea.

It's an awesome mission to contemplate. We know that the flak will be intense and accurate, and that the Luftwaffe will be out in force looking for quick-hitting opportunities. We need to call on all our inner resources to prepare for what lies ahead. Before we attack we must fight our own internal battles.

My luck has finally caught up with me. We missed one raid over Berlin because we hadn't returned from our R and R leave in Scotland. Our field at Polebrook lost six planes on that mission. We flew that afternoon to a landing strip on the east coast of England to pick up Lieutenant Hibbard and what was left of his crew, their plane having been turned into a ragged sieve that still, somehow, could fly.

We'd also prepared ourselves for another raid on Berlin, but the mission was scrubbed at the last moment. We endured the agony of thinking we were going, worked on ourselves psychologically to ease our apprehensions and then had the mission called off because the Germans found out about it. We had lost the element of surprise.

I remember how we stood around the plane, waiting for the signal to board the crews and start our engines. The crew chief dressed in his fatigues and baseball cap lounged around with us, making sure, even up until the last moment, that the plane was ready to fly. I was on edge, my nervousness turning into silliness—making cracks and laughing. I picked up a small square of metal, holding it this way and that, pretending it was a shield warding off chunks of flak as they flew at us from all angles over Berlin. The crew had chuckled at my childishness, relaxing a little because of it.

Scrubbing the mission deflated me, like air being gradually let out of a balloon. I came down off a psychological high point, slowly returned to my ordinary life. I changed from being a keyed-up warrior to a regular human being.

But this is a different day. We take off at close to 1100 hours, late for a mission of this scope, the sky hazy and streaked with cirrus. We leave the English coast flying at only 5000 feet, but soon begin our climb out over the North Sea. We have two hours of flying time before we reach the Danish coast, two hours without much to do except think about the mission ahead.

The gray-blue emptiness of the North Sea seems to go on forever. We fly in the lead box today, right off the wing of the lead plane. Other groups fly in front of us and behind; flocks of metal birds. Time passes slowly.

As we finally near the Danish coast, an ominous line of clouds appears ahead. The closer we approach, the more formidable it looks. It's a huge barrier of fibrous bulging cumulus clouds and well-developed thunderheads, their filmy anvils spreading out along the front. Their tops tower above us, perhaps to 35,000 feet, higher than we can fly. The first group flies right into it, but soon retreats in disarray, their planes scattered. The word goes out from the mission commander that the clouds are seething with severe turbulence, and that we have no way to go through it, around it or above it. We'll have to abort the mission. Flak batteries on Denmark's Sylt and Amurm Islands fire on us, but their bursts are few and off the mark.

We bank slowly to the left, turning in a wide circle until we're on course back to England. Again I'd steeled myself for the mission, and now it wouldn't happen. I rein in my apprehensions and begin to relax. Bad weather saved the day for the armament factory— and perhaps for a number of us who might have been lost.

I can't understand why the meteorologists didn't know about the squall line as they had flown weather planes over Germany regularly to monitor atmospheric conditions. Perhaps the cold front had intensified since their last observations. It seems to me that the mission had been an incredible waste of money and energy to be stopped by a weather disturbance they should have known about.

I think again about my incredible good fortune, or that God must be watching over me. As we descend over the North Sea, I replace the pins in my 500-pound bombs. I missed one raid to Berlin because I was on leave, avoided another when the mission was scrubbed, and now I've dodged one more because of weather.

We roar in over the English coast at only 2500 feet, the green fields, hedgerows and forests flashing by beneath us, on a beeline for Polebrook. We land just after 1530 hours. We're overjoyed that we're to be credited with a mission since we touched enemy territory, were fired upon and flew for just over four hours. What began as a dangerous mission turned into an easy one—with the same credit. But the scales tend to balance—the next mission could be deadly.

HAIR

"What are your folks gonna think when they see that you're losing your hair, eh?" asks Podoske as I sit on my bunk.

Sensitive about the subject, I don't answer him. He keeps it up.

"You know, you're really losing it around your temples and the back of your head where you can't see it."

"Cut it out, Podoske."

Sensing that he really has me worried, that I'm upset, he goes on teasing me with a sinister smile on his face, as though he enjoys needling me.

"Yeah. What's your girlfriend gonna say when she sees you? What about that? You're gonna go home losing your hair, and they're all gonna know it."

I should have been angry with him, but instead I roll into a psychological ball of melancholy, the pillbug routine. He's never treated me this way before. Maybe he's known me too long. Maybe he's just sick of being around me. I worry about losing what one of our neighbor women had called my "crowning glory," but I also wonder about him. He's not himself. Perhaps our missions are wearing him down so that he needs to fight back anyway he can.

Even without Podoske's remarks I'd been concerned about my hair, having noticed from looking into the mirror each day that it was beginning to thin at the temples. I wrote home about it:

"One thing I never wanted to do was lose any of it. Flying doesn't agree with my hair for some

reason. *Hair oil is almost impossible to get, and I haven't had any for about two weeks. In the cities they have some Brylecreem which is England's standard hair dressing, and I believe the only one here. I guess I'll have to go to town to get some."*

Many of the men in our barracks are having the same problem. Some have already lost most of theirs even though they're only in their twenties. Sometimes we talk about the possible cause. The pilot in the bunk across from me who's totally bald except for a little downy fringe around the edges, claims that he washed his hair too often, that he had literally rubbed it away, but another says he lost his because he didn't shampoo it enough. A navigator blames the dryness of high altitude flying; while I think that the tight flying helmets we wear cause it by cutting off the blood supply to the scalp. Some say it's heredity, but my father and his father have thick heads of hair.

Later I write home again:

"Yes, my hair is still getting a little thin in a spot or two. I can't help but worry about it, but I don't think it's too serious. Over my right temple is the only bad spot. I think it's from wearing army hats. I shampoo once or twice a week. I wonder if you could send me some olive oil for my hair. My scalp is dry, and I think that would be pretty good oil for it. I'm pretty lucky. Some fellows have lost almost all of their hair.

I bought a hair dressing from one of the chemist shops in Peterborough, a highly perfumed creamy mixture that I hesitated to try. The first time I used it coincided with our only days of hot weather, a balmy period that aroused all the bees, wasps and other insects. Wasps even landed on our food in the mess hall. A few officers had been stung. As I walked to lunch bees came to me from everywhere, buzzing around my head as though I were some huge walking flower. I flailed my arms to protect myself, but my fragrant tonic was driving them wild. I survived the walk to and from chow without being stung, but I washed the stuff out of my hair immediately and never used it again.

I, like so many others, used Vitalis, an alcohol-based hair tonic that we also found would start our coal fires in the potbellied stove. We would soak the black lumps with it, close the small iron door for a few moments, open it and throw in a lighted match. The alcohol fumes ignited with a pale blue explosion that gradually started the fire. The smells of Vitalis and of burning coal are the fragrances I most associate with the base, and I liked them both.

I write once more:

"You know, I would like some dried fruit and also some Pabst cheese. We have a lot of Ritz crackers, but no cheese to go on them. If you can get hold of any, we would sure appreciate it. I guess I already mentioned the olive oil."

Somehow I believe that olive oil will restore my scalp, supply a lubricant to keep it moist and prevent my hair from falling out. I thought about the Greeks and Romans who used it to add brilliance and texture to theirs. I had faith in this time-honored remedy.

My parents write me about Bob Anderson, how he had aged in the service. I reply:

"When I first got in the army, people thought I didn't look old enough to be in the army. Now people constantly guess my age as four or five years older than I actually am, and are surprised when I tell them my age [19]. I haven't noticed any difference except in my hair. It has receded slightly, as I have told you. I'm so very worried about it. I'm too young to lose any, and I hope what the pharmacist said was true, that some of it will grow back. I guess it came out with nervousness or something. I'll swear I aged a whole year during a single raid sometimes."

I wait for the olive oil, the magic restorer, and finally receive it.

After shampooing I work a little of the oil into my hair, massaging it in with my fingers, their tips glistening among my thinning waves. It's really ludicrous to worry about losing my hair when losing my life is an almost daily possibility, but I cling to the idea that there will be life after combat, and the way I look will play a significant role in that life. We'll have to see what the olive oil will do.

CHARLES N. STEVENS

THE KRUPP SUBMARINE WORKS AT KIEL

Flying out over the flat vastness of the North Sea becomes routine after a while, and a bit monotonous. Today, a solid blanket of clouds lies over the sea, white oblivion as far as I can see. Two numbing hours lie ahead before we cross the German coast. The engines drone as we slowly climb, whirring, humming, their sound mesmerizing. I'm suspended in the emptiness before us, in the plane's steady monotone. The intercom is quiet. I sit on my small bombardier's seat before my picture window, running my eyes across the formless mists below. It's early afternoon, and I'm drowsy.

In the bomb bay we carry five 1000-pound bombs, hard, cold olive-drab cylinders wearing two yellow bands. The sharp metal fins of the missiles point back, their tapered noses bearing small aluminum propellers like children's bright whirligigs. They're destined for the Krupp Submarine Works at Kiel on the Baltic Sea. Perhaps we can slow down the building of subs that attack our convoys in the Atlantic and North Sea. The city also is the location of the largest and most important navy base in Germany as well as the famous Kiel Canal connecting to the Elbe River.

We turn toward the southeast now on a direct line toward the north German coast, a heading that would take us, if we followed it all the way, to Hamburg. We keep the enemy guessing about our target.

A flak barrage flecks the sky over Bremen as we pass near it, the gunners letting us know they're ready for us if we have any intention of coming closer. I begin to think more about the mission, begin to feel it physically—the tightening of the anal sphincter, the sinking feeling in the stomach as though I had just descended in a fast elevator, a gentle roiling of the intestines, a strange twisting in the testicles, tension in the muscles.

On previous missions my gastrointestinal system had bothered me more than the other afflictions, an emotional diarrhea that I could do nothing about except pray and trust the power of my sphincter muscle. There are no bathrooms on a B-17; there is nowhere to go. Besides the emotion of combat, we must contend with the low pressure of high altitude, a condition that compounds the effect of higher pressure within our bodies. B-17s are not pressurized. Looseness of the bowels is common around the target areas. A few airmen aren't able to withstand the pressure, having to let it go, suffering the consequences. Thank God it had never happened to me.

When I feel my innards churning, writhing inside like fat thin-skinned snakes, the discomfort building, I imagine the toilet back at the base, suddenly yearning for it. I think about its porcelained loveliness, its shadowed enclosure. All is quiet and hushed and safe there, and I alone, without a single other voice to be heard, am able to use it in perfect peace.

Redheaded Knoop, a navigator in our squadron, unable to control his urge, had used a spread-out newspaper as a toilet. Afterwards he folded up the corners and took the package to the bomb bays. He attempted to rid himself of it by tossing it out of the open doors. Thinking it would drop away smoothly like a bomb, he quickly faced reality, the icy gusts blasting in shredding the package, plastering tatters of paper and its vile contents all over him and the bomb bay.

The other function had been easier, although not at first. Unable to contain myself any longer during a flight, I had to unplug my heated suit, disconnect my oxygen hose, clamping it immediately to a small portable oxygen bottle, and unsnap my intercom connection to prepare for the short but long journey to the bomb bay where a relief tube hung near the catwalk. Creeping clumsily in my flying suit with its layers of equipment, clutching the small cylinder, I made my way through the nose, squeezed through the pilot's compartment, and nudged around the engineer's turret to the bomb bay. As I must hold the spare oxygen bottle with one hand, I had only the other to work with. The relief tube was nothing more than a funnel with a long piece of rubber tubing leading out of the airplane. After taking a long time to get to what I want through my layers of clothing, I attempted to use the tube. All was well at first, but then the liquid froze in the tube. I had to stop, letting it slowly drain out of the funnel. By the time I reached the nose of the plane, I vowed that I would never go through the trouble again.

I learned that most airmen carry a screw-top jar, emptying the contents when they returned. Our crew chief supplied me with one, solving my problem.

After approaching Hamburg, we veer toward the northeast, toward our target at Kiel. The Hamburg gunners put up a stiff barrage, but we skirt their main defenses. I slip into my flak vests and don my helmet.

Clouds still mask all the land beneath us, some of the cumulus tops rising to over 21,000 feet. Below the clouds, down in Kiel, it must be a gloomy, gray wet afternoon, and now they're about to suffer the pounding of their submarine works. Our bombing will have to be done by radar. We throw out chaff, the aluminum "icicles" that create a metallic cloud, giving the German gunners a false picture on their radar screens. They launch a murderous barrage, most of it far to the left of us. I check my intervalometer to make sure it's set on train, the bombs to fall 150 feet apart on the ground, then watch the lead plane through the slit between my helmet and flak vests. Some of the flak begins to burst among us. We fill the sky with 1000-pound and 500-pound bombs, dribbling them out in a wide swath. After bombing, we cut to the north, out over the Baltic then bank west for the trip home. All our planes have made it through.

We had had two radar bombing planes with us at first. One of them aborted the mission early because of engine trouble. The second one, our lead plane, developed problems with the radar set, the "Mickey", the whole system failing just 20 minutes before the target. The lead bombardier then aimed his bombs on the smoke markers still persisting from the group ahead of us. But the long arching trails tracing the path of his bombs down to the clouds can drift in the wind, and how accurate had the drop from the group ahead been in the first place? Our bombs might have only churned up the Baltic for all we know.

About halfway home we turn in a wide circle to the left, completing a broad circular path down through the clouds. We fly under them all the way back to England, zooming in over the coast near Crowmer at only 2000 feet. We'd been away for over seven and one-half hours, and are not really sure we hit anything.

RAIN AND RUMORS

Out on the lonely hardstands, rainwater runs in rivulets down the aluminum wings and bodies of our bombers. It beads on the Plexiglas, coalescing drops running down in quick little rivers. Rain drips from their cold skins, dribbles on the concrete below, blends with thin coatings of oil and grease. Soft veils of mist and wisps of fog dim the planes parked farthest away.

Inside the barracks we gather around the thrumming coal stove, talking, writing letters, washing out underclothes. Rain streaks the windows, the gray gloom of the low clouds smothering the light that usually pours through them. We've been grounded by the weather for four days, and the base meteorologists expect more storminess. Our inactivity has made us all fidgety or bored. We curse the rain because it prevents us from completing our missions and going home, but at the same time we welcome it because it keeps us away from the danger of flying them.

Out of the murkiness, a rumor spreads through the barracks like a fast-moving brush fire. Crews with a certain number of missions will be sent home, their tours of duty considered complete. With our 29 missions, we might qualify. The story, stated as fact, an official policy, sounds too good to be true, but with all my heart I want to believe it. I've learned, however, not to trust rumors, having seen many good ones dissolve in the past. I embrace this one because I want to. All of a sudden the rain and cold don't mean much to me because I'm warm inside with the glow of going home. I stop worrying about missions. I thank

God for pulling me through. I float in a levity I hadn't known for months.

After five days of wet, unsettled weather, the sun finally breaks through, but its luster is tarnished by the news that what we had understood as fact only the day before is now uncertain. It still might be true, but my hopes for it begin to fade. I can't enjoy the sun. I'd felt that I was free, that my days of flying through the wretched flak were over, but now the high command, like some grotesque hand was about to snatch me back and plop me right down in the middle of the action again. I sadly write home that the good news I had written about the day before may not have any validity at all. We would have to wait and see, and I would have to deal with the uncertainty.

Like my morale, the weather deteriorates; the skies cloud over again, another dose of English weather. The new formula for the number of missions required comes down from headquarters. The official number one must fly has been raised from 30 to 35, but those crews who are nearly finished will be given a certain number of bonus missions. We are awarded one, so we must fly 34 of them. Instead of being finished as I had thought several days before, we have five more to fly.

Even though the news is bad, at least I know where I stand. I can deal with certainty. Now I wish the weather would clear again so we can begin to cross off our last five missions.

We had eight days of miserable weather. Never had we waited so long in between flights, never had we had to fill up so much idle time. We'd caught up on all our letter writing and washing, had even seen one movie twice at the base theater.

My undisciplined thoughts turn to home again. I think about the wonderful apple pies my mother made. I see a thick wedge of it in a bowl, doused with heavy cream. I think I would give a month's pay for a slice of it. I think about fresh cantaloupes for breakfast, scooping out succulent little hemispheres of their flesh with my spoon.

My parents had asked about the meals served on the base, so I had described one of our better suppers—"steak, mashed potatoes and gravy, peas and carrots, and macaroni. It really hit the spot, and I was so hungry at the time that it was pitiful." Even the tension of flying had never dulled my appetite.

We'd gone to church on Sunday. So many men attended the service that extra chairs had to be brought in. Being there is still very satisfying to me. I enjoy singing the same hymns that we had sung at home and listening to the reassuring words of the chaplain.

We listen to the radio, the American Forces Network. They always provide us with the latest news about the progress of the war. Each day our ground troops advance in France, and each gain brings us closer to the end of the war. They play our favorite records, especially "I'll Walk Alone" and "Lili Marlene." "Lili Marlene" intrigues me not only because of its haunting melody and its poignant words, but also because it had originated in Germany and is very popular among their troops. Men fighting on opposite sides love the same song because it speaks to each man's dream of returning from the war and being with his girl again.

The weather finally breaks, blue sky and sun peeping through the clouds, and the word travels that there's a mission on tomorrow. Five more to go! We're anxious to finish.

LUDWIGSHAVEN

Lumbering down the runway with our burden of six 1000-pound bombs and 2500 gallons of fuel, we struggle to gain enough speed for take-off. Nearing the end of the runway, our engines pulling with all their power, our plane reluctantly becomes airborne. I instinctively raise my feet when we streak over a line of treetops that I think we're going to brush. I'm sure we scatter a few leaves and twigs.

The weather is our first enemy of the day. The meteorologists had explained at the briefing that we'd have to fly up through several cloud layers, the higher ones posing the danger of rime icing. We flutter through low cumulus clouds, then nose up into the thickening gray altostratus layers, losing ourselves in their murkiness. Being suspended in the shadowy fog with no up or down, no reference points, is lonely and unsettling. Johnston has to be a firm believer in his instruments. We begin to pick up thin coatings of ice that set up vibrations in the plane, but our deicing boots on the wings function well.

Finally at 13,000 feet we emerge into the light of morning, the sun beaming down through scattered cirrus on a sea of fluffy white clouds cupped with gray shadows. We begin to assemble over the King's Cliff buncher as we look for the identifying flare colors for our group.

By ten o'clock we head out over the channel, now having climbed to 17,000 feet, the clouds below breaking into swelling cumuli that nearly reach our altitude. I settle back and think about the mission. Our target is the I. G. Farbin chemical plant at Ludwigshaven, in southwest Germany along the Rhine River. Our briefing officer had warned us that the target would be well defended. I begin to imagine the worst.

After passing over the French coast, we take an almost easterly course toward our objective still one and one-half hours away. I try to concentrate on the turreted beauty of the clouds below, their softness, shape and shadow patterns. This mission would be the first of our last five, and it promises to be a particularly rough one. After the rumor that had spread through the barracks that our missions might be over, I had thought I was home free, but here I am back at it. This would be one more mission out of the way.

As we near Ludwigshaven, the clouds below merge with a number of fibrous thunderhead tops rising up slightly higher than our 26,000 feet. At times we fly through their filmy translucence, our thick vapor trails adding to the surrealistic drama of our passing. The temperature outside is -38 degrees Centigrade. Veering off toward the northeast, we point ourselves directly toward the target. I check my flak vests, helmet, parachute and bomb settings. Up ahead, a seething conflagration of flak blackens the sky, the worst I had seen in a long while. I silently repeat the 23rd Psalm and prepare to fly into the German barrage. I open the bomb bay doors and watch the lead plane, trying to concentrate on that rather than the flak. The usual black explosions from 88 mm guns make up most of their fire, but among them are larger white ones with an insidious pinkish tint to them, strangely a blush of some beauty, bursts of heavy 105 mm shells. They're throwing up everything they have at us. Four Messerschimitt 210 twin-engine interceptors trail us near the target but never attack, probably wary of their own antiaircraft fire or looking for stragglers.

Their deadly accurate flak continues to bloom among us, vicious blasts that thump over the roar of our engines and flash in the thin blue sky, filling the space we must fly through with flying shrapnel that rips at our formation. I know we're taking hits. At last the bombs from the lead plane drop. I release mine. I close our bomb bay doors as we bank sharply to the left in an attempt to break free of their dogging fire.

Soon after making the turn Johnston's voice comes over the interphone.

"Pilot to crew. Is everyone okay? Check in with me one at a time."

A few moments later he says, "Podoske's been hit. Witherspoon, grab an oxygen bottle, and come up here. Bring the belts and see if you can stop his bleeding. Stevens and Warren, as soon as you can, take him down into your compartment so that he can lie down."

I'm stunned by his injury. We don't know how badly he's hurt. He'd been my best friend since our crew training in Louisiana. Again Johnston gets on the intercom.

"Podoske's been hit in the upper thigh. We don't know how deep the wound is. I asked him if he was okay. He gave me a high sign that he was. A minute later he passed out. He slumped over with his full weight on his control column. Lucas struggled to pull him off it."

Lucas and Warren and I help lower Podoske into our compartment. The shrapnel had ripped a long jagged gash in his flying suit. Blood from the wound soaks into the cloth. Shaken and pale, but now conscious, he sits on the floor. He's leaning back towards the pilot's compartment, his oxygen mask connected to a spare bottle.

At least our riddled plane is still flying. With all four engines still purring rhythmically, we know our chances are good for keeping up with the formation. Our box, the lead, had caught the brunt of the anti-aircraft fire. Several of our planes are struggling. One severely damaged plane, Lieutenant Shera's, drops out of formation. Then another slips back, unable to keep up, the pilot, Lieutenant Barker, radioing that he hoped to make it to Allied-occupied France.

I gradually become aware that I'm light-headed, as though I'm about to black out. Remembering my cadet training in Houston, I check the color of my fingernails. They are all turning blue, a sign of anoxia. Apparently my oxygen lines or regulators had been damaged. I quickly connect my mask to a spare portable bottle, inhaling deeply on full oxygen until I recover.

Soon after flying away from the target, and after we had lowered our altitude to 17,000 feet, we approach a line of towering thunderheads, their feathery anvils spread out high against the sky like ghostly children, their arms locked together, jeering, telling us we shall not pass. We turn abruptly south to avoid them, hoping we can find a way around the menacing wall. Podoske still looks shaken but doesn't seem to be in critical condition.

After climbing again to 26,000 feet we maneuver an end run around the worst of the thunderheads then resume flying toward England. Near Paris we begin a steep descent by S'ing back and forth down through the clouds to get under the weather. After lowering to nearly 8000 feet, we remove our oxygen equipment. The pressure in my spare bottle had become quite low. Snapping off our wet rubbery masks, we immediately sigh and breathe fully again like normal human beings.

Podoske wants a cigarette right away, something to calm his nerves. Warren lights it for him, and the navigator's compartment fills with blue curls of smoke and the sweet acrid scent of tobacco. Podoske speaks weakly.

"My intestines are writhing around. Maybe the shrapnel got all the way to my guts. A chunk might have lodged in or close to my testicles. My God, I hope not."

He blows great puffs of smoke that tumble around inside the nose of the plane. Fears of what might have happened to him grip Podoske. Warren and I try to console him. He bears the pain of his wound bravely.

Near Paris we break through the lower clouds at only 2000 feet. I think about our first mission to Paris just three months before. Even at our high altitude then, the German flak gunners had taken their toll. Now we fly low unmolested, a good measure of how far the Allied troops had advanced across France.

We fly even lower, skimming across France almost at tree top level. It's a quick trip over the devastation of a war zone. Bomb craters and shell holes nearly filled with muddy rainwater pock the farmlands and rural backyards. Here and there farmhouses lie in ruins, their ancient stones scattered by the mayhem of modern war. Women with kerchiefs tied around their heads and men wearing thick rustic trousers and coats, farmer's caps on their heads, wave at us as we fly over. I can almost see the expressions on their faces as they look up, enveloped in the thunder of our formation.

Near the channel and over it we pass through numerous showers, the rain blasting against the Plexiglas, the quivering rivulets creeping across it, the other planes dimmed in the rain. Weather had been our second enemy all day, and it's having its last fling before we settle back to earth again. After flying by the Polebrook control tower and firing red flares with our Very pistol to let them know we have wounded aboard, we land at shortly after four in the afternoon, touching down in a cold slanting shower driven by a brisk northwest wind. The ambulance meets our plane. They remove Podoske's torn and bloody flying suit and lay him carefully on a stretcher that they slip into the ambulance.

* * *

We are saddened to hear that one of our planes, Lieutenant Haba's, had crashed near Market Deeping during our assembly over England before we had left for the mission. No one had survived the crash except the tail gunner. Cause of the mishap is unknown, but since many planes had had problems with icing as they climbed through the clouds, that could have been it.

The two planes that had left our formation over Germany because of flak damage have not been heard from and are presumed lost.

Two more of our planes wounded by flak had managed to get back across the channel, but could not reach our base, having to set down at Tangmere near the coast.

* * *

Battle damage to our ship, airplane No. 43-37696, 509th Squadron:

"Flak hole through right elevator. Flak hole underside right stabilizer. Two flak holes underside right wing, damaging oil and tokio tanks. Flak hole #3 nacelle, damaging ring and cowl bracket. Flak hole right side of fuselage below top turret. Flak hole right side of fuselage rear of navigator's compartment, damaging oxygen system, heated suit outlet and bracket for elevator pulley support."

Seven other planes had sustained major damage.

* * *

Johnston, Warren and I walk over to the base hospital the following day to visit Podoske. We take him some candy bars and cigarettes and ask about his condition. The shrapnel had penetrated deep into his thigh, lodging in the muscle very close to the main artery. Luckily it had missed the bone or any vital nerve. The wound hadn't affected his intestines or any part of his reproductive system as he'd feared.

Doctors operated on him the evening after we returned, removing a long jagged chunk of flak that he keeps in an envelope on a stand by his bed. Already he's unhappy about lying around with nothing to do, but the doctors want to keep him in the hospital for another month, a real trial for a man who craves being active. While we visit Podoske, I see several other people that I know lying in beds, all of whom had been wounded.

Again, after such a mission, I feel very fortunate to be walking around without pain and without a wound, not even a scratch. Four more missions, and I'm finished.

FIGHTER BAIT

"Fighter bait. That's all we are on this mission," complains one of the men as we walk out of the briefing room. "Just fighter bait."

I hadn't given the mission such a quaint name, but I have to agree with him. The briefing officer hadn't put it that way, but it's exactly what he meant.

"We're going to head out over the North Sea," he said. "Then we'll fly southeast on a course between Hamburg and Kiel toward Berlin. We'll skirt around it on the east side. Flying close to the major cities should bring out the Luftwaffe, and that's what we want to do—flush 'em out and shoot 'em down. When they come for us, our gunners and the Mustangs will knock 'em out. The Luftwaffe is alive and well, and it's our job to destroy it."

Our target is ostensibly the oil storage tanks and facilities at Ruhland, Germany, south of Berlin, but clearly our other purpose is to draw up enemy fighter planes. No one likes the mission except the strategists in their comfortable headquarters. We had a similar mission before and hadn't appreciated it either. I feel used, as though I'm expendable, as if I'm only a number, a statistic. We grumble, but go about our business preparing for the raid.

It's still early morning as we troop to the armament shack to pick up our guns, the sun having just risen on a scattered flotilla of cumulus clouds floating in a light haze. The cool smell of dew and earth lingers in the air. We may be all right on the mission if it goes well, but if there are any screw-ups or lapses in cover by our fighter support, the Luftwaffe might be able to sneak in for a quick attack. Despite the honor of sacrificing myself for the greater strategic interest of the war, I personally don't want the fighters to come up. I'm no warrior. I have no desire to be heroic or legendary or to cover myself with glory, but if the German boys hit us head-on, I'll empty my chin turret guns on them. I'm exhausted. I want to go home.

We growl and walk around grimly, but go out to our planes and prepare for the mission, keeping our private thoughts to ourselves. Lieutenant Hibbard will be our co-pilot today in place of Podoske who must remain in the hospital for a month. Most of Hibbard's crew had bailed out over Germany on a raid to Berlin, so now he fills in wherever he's needed. I like him very much, and I'm glad to have him with us.

Out over the familiar expanses of the North Sea we begin our slow climb, planning to reach 20,000 feet by the time we pass over enemy territory. The flight over open water should be simple, a nearly straight path to the Danish Peninsula. Several times I notice we're changing course, angling out then coming back when we should be flying straight.

"Bombardier to pilot."

Two clicks.

"Why are we zigzagging like this?"

"Yeah. The combat wing in front of us is flying too slow. We jog out to cover more distance, to stay behind them."

Two clicks.

We'd never had this problem before, and I'm uncomfortable. A sense of foreboding settles over me like a cold mist. By the time we reach the peninsula, we're back on course behind the slow-moving formations ahead.

Flying over German territory now between Hamburg and Kiel, we still have seen no sign of the Luftwaffe and very little flak. We fly in the lead box at 28,000 feet, the high box above us and behind, the low below, 36 of us, 12 in a box, in good tight formation.

Just northeast of Berlin we again face the problem of overtaking the sluggish groups ahead of us, the ones that should bomb the target before we do. We turn sharply to the right to lose ground so that we'll not overrun them. It's dangerous to deviate much from course over Germany, especially near Berlin that is so heavily defended. Our evasive turn will take us right into their flak defenses. I'm nervous about it.

We veer to the left to avoid the antiaircraft fire from the capital, then resume our original course, but as we do, a chaotic mix-up of groups begins. Some pass up others, while a few squadrons, trying to avoid flak, sweep across the flight paths of others. Another group filters through our low box, scattering our planes, effectively breaking up the formation, leaving them vulnerable to interceptors.

Nearing the bomb run now, the confusion and disorder continues. We turn in a great circle to allow another group to bomb ahead of us, but by the time we resume the run, we're cut off by still another flight of bombers. Finally our box gets a try at the target, not the original one of the oil facilities at Ruhland, but a large aluminum plant 10 miles from there, the Lauta Aluminum Works of the Vereinigte Aluminum Werke. German gunners fire at us, but their flak is largely ineffective.

In the chaos of taking turns to bomb, and trying to stay out of each other's way, even our own boxes become separated. I suddenly realize that ours is flying all by it self, just twelve of us with no other bombers around. We're on course, but we're alone without a fighter escort deep in the heart of Germany. It's only a matter of time until the Luftwaffe picks up our isolated formation. I'm very tense. The bandits are active today. An attack could come at any moment.

Far ahead of us and to the right German fighters rip into another scattered formation. It's a macabre party with confetti and streamers of flame and black smoke as they down one plane after another. I watch the gruesome spectacle from afar, but I ache for those men and what they must be going through. I feel that the same fate is in store for us. My saliva dries up, and my tongue begins to stick to the roof of my mouth.

"Pilot to crew. Be alert. We've radioed for a fighter escort, and they've responded, but as you can see, they're not here yet."

I scan the sky for enemy planes and our protectors. We'd never been in such a precarious situation before. We tighten up our formation, tucking our wings in as closely as possible to each other, concentrating our firepower.

Finally a whole squadron of P-51 Mustangs arrives, silver, sleek and beautiful, flying just above us. Their appearance is like the cavalry charging over the hill with bugles blowing, rescuing a beleaguered group of pioneers at the very last moment, just before they are about to be wiped out. I begin to relax. I admire the clean lines of the Mustangs, the raw power of their engines, even their squared-off wing tips. Some of them might have been built at the North American Aviation plant in my hometown of Inglewood. I'm indebted to those pilots out there and the security of their protective shield. Without them we might have been eliminated by now.

We'd bombed the target just after noon, now at close to 1500 hours we cross the Belgian coast and let down across the channel. It had been a long mission, one full of doubts and tensions. We zoom over the English coast at 5000 feet, landing at Polebrook just before 1600 hours.

* * *

Only after we return to the field do we learn about the full extent of what had happened on the mission. When squadrons of German fighters flying in formation had attacked our scattered low box near Berlin, they'd downed six of our bombers, all in just one pass. Most had exploded when they were hit, and only one parachute had been observed. We'd lost bombers piloted by Lieutenants Adams, Lopert, Schoenian, Schmollinger, Brown and Hadley along with their crews, ten men to a plane. One of the surviving pilots said, "We were in good formation until the wing ahead of us flew a collision course into us after taking evasive action from flak. Our formation was broken up, and we were duck soup for the fighters who attacked immediately." One plane had also been shot down from our high box, Lieutenant Hennigan's. Seventy of our men would not return to the base. Another barracks emptied out.

Only the lead box, ours, had hit a target, the secondary one at Lauta. The high box, seeking a target of opportunity in the confusion had dropped their load on the city of Plauen, most of the bombs falling on the outskirts of the town where very little damage was done. The low box, with only six planes left out of twelve, had accidentally released theirs when the deputy lead bombardier thought he saw a signal flashed from the lead plane. It turned out to be merely the reflection of the sun off of the Aldis lamp. The bombs landed in fields at least three miles from the target. After the very long mission, the extent of our losses and the grave danger, it had hardly been worth it.

I also talk to a radio operator who had flown with us in our box, a man who speaks German and monitors their fighter channels.

"Yeah, they knew we were out there by ourselves. They were scrambling fighters from every airfield in the area to come up and take care of us. That's when I told the lead ship that we'd better call for fighter support in a hurry. When the P-51s arrived, they called off the air strike against us."

What I had feared was happening, was happening—we'd been on the verge of being ambushed, perhaps annihilated like the other group I'd seen in the distance.

Another piece of luck, a roll of the dice, a stroke of cosmic fortune, a case of God looking out for me—whatever the cause, I'd squeaked through again. Had we been in the low box today, we might not have made it. If the Mustangs had not arrived, we might not have escaped either.

Fighter bait. That is what we'd been—the lures for vicious fish that had swallowed some of us while, I imagined, the gentlemen back in headquarters sipped steaming coffee out of thick mugs and pored over their statistics.

RECOGNITION

After the numbing tension and fatigue of the last mission, all I'd been able to think of was the sack. I'd slipped into a deep sleep within minutes, and had had to be roused at ten o'clock the next morning. I might have slept far into the afternoon had Warren not jostled me out of my dreams.

I am still logy, as though I'd been drugged, and the dull aches and sniffles of a developing cold add to my discomfort. A typhus shot has given me a touch of fever and an increasingly sore arm. A boil forming on my back had bothered me on the last mission when my heavy flak vests had irritated it. In my foggy mood I feel like Job being tested for the strength of his faith.

A sergeant walks into our barracks with four small dark blue cases, and asks for Johnston.

"Congratulations sir", he says as he hands the cases to him. "These are Distinguished Flying Crosses for the officers on your crew."

We set Podoske's case aside, and open our own. The red, white and blue ribbon gradually tapers down to a gleaming silver medal with two slightly raised crossed propellers on it. It is beautiful. I look at it for a long time, studying it, turning it this way and that. It brightens my morale, and brings me out of my lethargy. It is our reward for having completed thirty missions, the thirtieth one being the mission to Ludwigshaven where Podoske had been wounded.

Even though I'm happy about earning the medal, its true significance to me is that our tour of duty is nearly over. We have only three more missions left. I feel both proud and lucky—proud because I had had the personal strength to endure thirty of them and lucky because I had not been shot down or injured. Many other deserving men had been shot down before they reached their thirtieth mission, and would never receive the honor.

As with the Air Medal that had been presented to us after completing seven missions, the Distinguished Flying Cross had been awarded automatically. I had done nothing "special" to earn it except endure the rigors of war and, of course, survive.

None of us is heroic like the fearless characters that exist in war and adventure movies or novels, all of which are larger than life. Their actions are "condensed" so that we learn about only a small part of their lives, perhaps only a few moments of it, the strong heroic part that is in turn exaggerated and romanticized. Very few people in or out of the war are ever like them.

Ours is a quiet, day-by-day fortitude sustained over a long period of time, the kind that emerges out of stamina and commitment, of performing our jobs professionally in the face of odds. As in all wars and in all branches of the armed service, action is sporadic with periods, sometimes long ones, between skirmishes. Out of the one hundred days or so that I had been at Polebrook, thirty-one of them had been spent flying, seventy not—time for leaves, recuperation and rest, and training. On the missions themselves many hours had been spent assembling over England, crossing friendly territory or flying in relatively "safe" areas. With some glaring exceptions, most of the opposition from German flak and fighters had occurred near and over the targets, most of it for a matter of minutes, but it was during that short time span, the running of the gauntlet, that planes went down and crews were wounded. In a strange way we are like firemen who remain in the firehouse in perfect safety then have to go out occasionally to battle fires, some of which are dangerous or even life-threatening, situations that test their mettle.

Despite the briefness of flak barrages and attacks by fighters, those deadly minutes seem like hours, and the tensions involved are excruciating. Simply taking off with a full load of bombs and fuel is risky in itself, and the apprehensions of what lies ahead over enemy territory always weighs heavily on our minds.

Although there may have been true heroes on our base, in the motion picture sense of the term, I do not know of any. I am sure that at our field or any of the bomber bases there are men who have performed individual "heroic" acts, but most of us are simply young men caught up in the war who perform our duties well, who are able to climb into a bomber for each mission, face danger and live with the prospect of not coming back.

I don't know anyone who yearns to be a hero. Most men simply want to complete their missions, and go home. Most men do not want to be in precarious situations in which they, if they are lucky enough to survive, might become heroes or be expected to perform some gallant deed.

I don't know anyone who enjoys flying missions. Some of the innocent who at first think of the war as being a great adventure, who are eager for action, are usually cured after their first few trips through heavy flak. There may be a few who crave danger, who feel most alive when they live near the edge with their adrenalin pumping, but I personally do not know anyone like that in our barracks or on our base.

I don't know of anyone who hates the German people or gets pleasure out of bombing them. If they harbor such views, they are not expressed. We have all heard Nazi atrocity stories, and are familiar with the ruthless aggression of their leaders, but somehow we separate that from the ordinary citizen.

I know men who simply endure the clammy grip of fear, who pray to God to get them through. I know men who sink into the leaden heaviness of fatigue, who want nothing more than to sleep. I know men whose greatest joy is receiving a letter from home.

I look at the medal again, its bright ribbon and shiny silver propellers. I think back on all of the sweat and all of the trials I had been put through to get it. I am no movie hero, but I had earned the medal, and I cherish it.

STEIN'S MISSION

I'm surprised when Stein is made one of the lead bombardiers on a tactical mission to Holland. He'd arrived at the base weeks after me, and I'm disappointed that he'd been chosen instead. I say nothing about it, but I feel the slight just the same. From the beginning of our training, however, we'd agreed not to be a lead crew, thinking it would delay our rate of missions and our going home.

Today's mission would be different from any that we'd tried before. Instead of bombing in three boxes of twelve planes, each flying at different altitudes, we would attack in formations of from four to six planes at the same level, going after different targets in the area. For this operation more bombardiers using bombsights are needed. A German force of tanks, artillery and infantry had been massing in a forested area of Holland near Groesbeck. The Air Force had been called to inflict as much damage on them as possible, especially the tanks that had been lurking in the trees at the edge of the forest.

As we leave the English Channel and fly relatively low, just over 16,000 feet at the Belgian coast, I think about Stein again. His dry hair dark, his face, I thought, rather pale, what I called the Eastern look, he always wore a pleasant expression, his manner friendly but quiet. He'd sometimes stunned me with his tales of growing up in New York City.

"Did you ever play snake?" he'd asked me in his Brooklyn accent.

"I don't think so," I replied. "What is it?"

With a sly grin on his face, a crooked smile that makes me think he's about to tell me a "story" that will shock me, he'd said, "Well, when we were teen-agers, we'd get a group of boys and girls together then find some abandoned place where we wouldn't be seen. We'd take off our clothes, rub ourselves down with mineral oil, then all writhe together like snakes."

I had to decide whether to believe him or not. All through my time in the service, men had been telling me what they'd done as teen-agers. One fact was certain. His experiences, and those of most men at that age, had been vastly different from my own.

Still over Belgium, we turn sharply toward the northeast and our target in Holland. I'm uncomfortable with our lower than normal altitude as the flak will be more accurate. Flying in such small formations also seems strange. Between the scattered clouds, the targeted forest shapes appear through the haze. Flak begins popping among us, but our unusual arrangement seems to confuse the German gunners. The flak explosions come close though, near enough to inflict damage.

As I open the bomb bay doors, and we start on the bomb run, I notice a passenger train racing along the flat Dutch countryside close to the very woods where the German tanks are hiding. Steam billows from the locomotive and streams out behind, the thick rolling cloud persisting in the cool morning air.

The lead plane begins to release its 24 240-pound fragmentation bombs, one at a time, to land 100 feet apart on the ground. The rest of us immediately begin our bomb trains. I push my head forward to watch the results. Part of our impact pattern walks across the forest, but another portion straddles the railroad tracks, some of our load catching the hapless locomotive, the punctured boiler spewing plumes of steam in every direction, snorting like a wounded dragon, the brown earth lifting from explosions all around it.

At first I think we've been successful in destroying that speeding train, but on the way back, I begin to wonder about it. I hope that the train carried German soldiers rushing to the front rather than a Dutch express packed with civilians. Loving railroads and trains as I do, and writing regularly to a steam locomotive engineer on the Union Pacific, I begin to feel for his Dutch counterpart who probably hadn't survived.

The engineer had done his job, and I'd done mine. Stein, the man who had played "snake" in his youth, had done his. All of us are strangely and tragically brought together by the madness and sorrow of war.

A VOICE FROM THE PAST

With a plush mattress of clouds below us, we ease into a slow wide circle just off the English coast. Except for one flak-damaged bomber that had to ditch in the channel, all of us fly in the same gentle curve, thirty-five planes in formation, banking, gradually losing altitude. One more broad turn, and we'll sink into the silkiness.

Radio messages tell us that Polebrook is wrapped in a thick swath of clouds, rain and fog. We'll have to land at Hardwick, a B-24 base much closer to the coast than ours. A landing there will be feasible, at least at the present time, if we can get under the low ceiling.

Weather, the nemesis of bombing missions, had also hampered us over Germany where we were to blast the railroad yards at Soest, northeast of Cologne. Cirrus clouds and thick vapor trails from other groups obscured the target for the high and lead boxes, only the low box flying slightly beneath the clouds, able to sight on the marshalling yards. The lead box was locked in the translucent fuzziness of the cirrus while our plane as part of the high box skimmed over the wispy crystalline tops.

We'd flown on to Hamm, our secondary target, only to find the whole area obscured by clouds. German gunners found us, pummeling us with a moderate dose of accurate antiaircraft fire, knocking one of our planes out of formation. Black blobs had burst all through us until we finally flew out of range. They also pestered us at Munster on the way in.

The lead box found a "target of opportunity," the marshalling yards at Emmerich, but ours, fearing we were on a collision course with another group groping through the webs of clouds and contrails, decided not to attempt a bombing run, but to take our bombs back to the base.

Down through the soup now, we fly low under a ragged gray overcast, still maintaining our formations. With the lead plane homing in on the alternate base, we zoom over green fields and deeper green forests, the land somber under the darkening sky and scattered mist. Near the field, streaking over the treetops, their leaves a blur beneath us, we break up into groups of threes. As the lead plane banks tightly, we bank even tighter, our dipped right wing closer to the trees than I wish it to be, still carrying our three tons of bombs. G-forces flatten me into the bombardier's seat, seem to shove it up through me, the blood in my head sloshed to the other side of my brain, my brain pushed somewhere else in my skull, my body momentarily shortened. I thank God that Johnston is such a superb pilot.

Coming out of the turn, we peel off, stringing ourselves out into a regular landing pattern. Our plane touches down gently on the unfamiliar runway, taxis past idle B-24s, and finally stops on a broad tarmac with the other B-17s. We walk close to the B-24s, superbly performing airplanes that I think appear squat and ugly compared to ours.

Our crew had never had to land at another field before. It's odd to see the Liberators on the field, sitting on their hardstands like exotic birds on their nests, the thick green grass all around them, the threatening sky overhead. All the buildings are strange to me, and I don't know where anything is. Officers from the field lead us to the mess hall where we fall ravenously upon a meal.

Shortly after dinner an officer assigns the pilots and co-pilots to the barracks for an overnight stay, hoping they'll be able to fly the planes back to Polebrook the following day. They load the rest of us into a convoy of trucks that will return us to our base. I sit in front with our driver. We roll slowly over the dark undulating landscape on narrow wet roads. Raindrops spatter the windshield, and streak in front of the dimmed headlights.

* * *

The following afternoon, our plane returned to Polebrook, Johnston asks me to go out and remove any machine gun guts that are still on board. As the armament officer of the crew, that's my job.

I can see immediately that the guns in the ball turret are still in place. I don't think I'd ever removed them from that particular turret before. I begin to manipulate the guns, but the angle is bad, the leverage awkward. In order to reach for the back plate and pull it up, I adjust my body by nestling the barrel of the gun in my belly. The moment the cold steel touches me, the voice of my old gunnery instructor back at Laredo,

Texas, sounds in my mind—"If there's a round in the chamber, the gun will fire when you slide up the back plate." The gunners were all supposed to clear them, so I know that there's little chance that a cartridge is still lodged there. Just in case, I move to the side as I work on the back plate. As I carefully tug upwards on it— BAM!—a round goes off, like a cherry bomb followed by a whining zing as the bullet rips across the crew chiefs' tents and out onto the field.

Several men clad in green fatigues and crumpled hats rush out of their crew chief tents. Several jog toward me.

"What in the hell happened?" exclaimed one of them. "My God, what did you do? I heard that bullet sing right over my tent."

"I lifted the back plate, and the gunner had left a damn round in there, "I explain, embarrassed.

Luckily the bullet hadn't struck anyone or hit anything vital, but the crew chiefs, thinking they were safe from the flying bullets of the war, had to think again.

I feel sheepish and a little queasy. I remember my soft abdomen pushed against the gun muzzle. If I'd left it there, I'd be dead now. I imagine my death—bleeding profusely with a hole blown through my middle, my life seeping out on the concrete of the hardstand. "The irony of it all," the men might say. "He only had one more mission to go. My God, after surviving all that hell, the son of a bitch kills himself at his own field because of a stupid error."

I'm angry with the gunner who should have cleared his weapon, but Johnston and I decide not to berate him. I go over my "death" many times and chastise myself for my mental lapse. I try to put it behind me, but each time I run my hand over the softness of my belly, I live it all over again.

THE FINAL MISSION

Sitting in my small bombardier's seat, I make last minute preparations for the mission. I check my parachute. It's on the floor to my right. My heavy corduroy-covered flak suits lie near it, coiled and limp, my steel helmet close by. One last look at the armament. Strings of brass cartridges gleam in the dim light, perfect rows of them sweeping into my chin turret like flat metal snakes. The chances are that after this, I'll never again have to feel the weight of the flak suits tugging on my shoulders, never have to tuck them in between my legs. I'll never have to peer out from beneath my helmet at exploding antiaircraft shells, or check the rounds leading into my machine guns.

This is the mission I've been longing for, the 34th, my final one. Waiting for the starting of the engines, I breathe in the familiar smell of our plane, of my compartment, a heady indescribable scent of metal, rubber, plastic and oil. From the moment the mission was called, I'd been thinking—This is it—If I can just squeak through this one, it'll be all over—but the Germans will have one last chance at me—a crew can be shot down on its last try as well as any other—flak bursts had come so close so many times—antiaircraft gunners may be loading their 88's right now—one of the shells could explode in our laps, turn us into a fireball—oh, the irony of it all—after escaping 33 times, they get us on our 34th.

I try to keep my fears at bay, to go about the flight as though it's simply another mission. I look out through the Plexiglas at the clouds, a low gray overcast that has pressed down on us all morning. Haze and fog dim the ghostly forests around the field and mask the B-17s on the farthest hardstands. The whole field, including the planes and men, seems shrouded in a cold moist gloom, a chill breath that makes me think again. Is the weather a bad omen?

I'd hoped that my last mission would be a "milk run," a short raid over the channel to the occupied portion of France, but it's not. Our target today is the Land Armament Works at Kassel, Germany. Our bomb bays are loaded with 500-pound bombs, half general purpose and half incendiary. Not only do we plan to blow up the factory, but to burn it too, to set off explosions of their ammunition.

I'm a 19 year-old boy/man from Inglewood, California, from quiet, peaceful Brett Street where the wind sighs in the trees, and low clouds roll in off the ocean in the afternoons, where my room holds all my special pictures on its walls, where my mother and father live with all of their love for me. Yet I sit on top of all this potential mayhem, prepared to unleash it on the factory at Kassel, ready to face the wrath of enemy gunners who will try to stop me, who will dance with glee should they blow our craft into a puff of scrap metal.

We taxi out with the other planes, joining the single-file parade of bombers inching up to the runway in the gloom. I look out over the line of planes ahead of us, the spread of their metallic wings, their whirling props, one B-17 following another. After today I'd never have to see this sight again or feel the tension and uncertainty about what lies ahead.

With Podoske still in the hospital Hibbard is again our co-pilot.

In position now at the end of the runway, Johnston guns the engines. We begin our slowly accelerating thrust down the long strip, our bomber wrapped in the thunder and vibrations of all that energy. The concrete streaks by faster and faster beneath us, the engines straining mightily to propel our tons of gasoline and bombs. As usual I check the airspeed indicator, watching the needle climb. Suddenly the power slacks off. I don't understand it. We must have lost an engine. But Johnston had cut them all.

Even with our power shut down, we still plummet down the runway. Johnston must be using the brakes. The hazy end of the runway is coming up fast! Several trucks and a number of spectators from the base are parked or standing directly at the end, foolhardy men who like to watch the bombers take off just a few feet over their heads. As we bear down on them, the men scatter. Several jump into their trucks, quickly moving them away. By the time we reach the end everyone has dispersed. As the engines had had to work full bore to overcome our inertia of rest, our brakes now work to overcome our considerable inertia of motion. Rolling much slower now, but still with considerable speed, we flash by the end of the runway, rip through a small row of short hedges and out into a rough grassy area, our wheels thudding, our plane shaking. Other B-17s are parked nearby. Finally we stop, miraculously without hitting anything.

Shaken, we all emerge from the plane. Those of us not in the cockpit had missed an even higher drama during the aborted take-off.

"We lost an engine about halfway down the runway," says Johnston, taking me aside. "I wanted to cut off the power, but Hibbard didn't think we could stop. He wanted to try taking off with three engines. Hibbard wanted full throttles, I wanted no throttle at all. We struggled. Finally I reached out and hit Hibbard as hard as I could to get him away from the controls. Lucas helped by reaching in and pulling back the throttles. I didn't know if I could stop the plane or not, but I thought that any attempt to take off with three engines would have been too risky. I stood on the brakes with my full weight. At last we got the damned thing stopped."

We'd been a split decision away from possibly being incinerated in a massive fire of burning fuel and twisted wreckage out in the adjoining forest. Again I credit Johnston for saving our lives. His skill, coolness and quick thinking had brought us through a close call one more time. We might have been able to take off, but again, we may not have.

Despite our near-catastrophe, we're still scheduled to fly. A truck rolls up to our errant plane, ready to take us to a spare that's already loaded. We gather our equipment and scramble into the truck. In our hurry to reach the other plane so that we can take off quickly and join the formation, we have little time to think about what had just happened.

We nose up into the gloom, lose ourselves in it, and then burst through the tops into the sunlight. It seems strange being in this plane, one that we're not used to. We assemble with the other bombers around the Kings Cliffe buncher, gathering our group together at 11,000 feet, far above the clouds. Once in formation, we leave the English coast at Clacton, heading southeast toward Belgium. I try to keep the demons down, try to squelch thoughts about the awful irony of going down on our last mission, daring instead to think about the joy of going home.

Staying on roughly the same course, we skirt around the south end of the heavily defended Ruhr Valley, then turn sharply toward the north. Huge cumulus clouds swell up from below, but we fly far above most of them. Tangles of cirrus float above us. Unfortunately, we fly in the low box today, not a good position, the German gunners usually picking on the lower formations.

At the IP we turn toward the southeast again for the bomb run. Heavy clouds and haze obscure the target. Bombing will have to be done by radar, by the PFF operator. The Kassel defense gunners begin their firing, lobbing shells into our box and the lead box. I've seen worse flak, but these boys are accurate; one battery could get lucky. I open our bomb bay doors, the shells popping among us. The lead releases its bombs, a smoke marker falling with them drawing a thick trail, like a dirty animal's tail, down toward the clouds. Our box and the high drop our bombs on the path left by the smoke marker. Because of the murkiness below, we have no idea whether we've hit the armament factory. We can only hope that the radar man had been accurate.

We take evasive action after the bomb run, zigging and zagging until we are out of the flak. None of our planes is so badly damaged that the pilots can't maintain a tight formation. I may have endured my last flak barrage unless we run into some on the way home. Earlier, gunners at Koblenz and Wiesbaden had taken pot shots at us on the way in, so we had to be prepared for the unexpected.

I begin to feel an upwelling of good feeling. I truly might have just run through my last flak gauntlet, but we're still over Germany. From my window I spot a B-17 from another group, flying all by it self, lower in the haze. The plane seems to be under control, but it's obviously injured. As I look, it suddenly bursts into a large fireball, a great red-orange chrysanthemum of flame. I see nothing left of the plane afterwards. I see no parachutes. I'm sad about the crew. They'd left their field just as we had, but they wouldn't be returning. I don't know how many missions they had flown before. Perhaps this was to be their final one too.

I can't get the fireball out of my mind. Just as I'd begun to feel a mild euphoria about being finished with my missions, I had to witness that tragedy. I almost feel as though God is showing me what might have been—"Yes, you have gone through 34 missions unscathed. You have completed your tour, but you have been lucky. What you have just seen could have happened to you. Those men, all perished now, were no more or less sacred than you."

By the time we reach the English Channel at the Belgian coast, it's just after 1600 hours. Clouds and dirty haze choke the channel, but it has never looked so good to me. I shake the image of the ill-fated bomber and float on the ecstasy I had always felt after we had reached the channel safely. It's the same feeling that had always given me the strength to fly the next mission.

It's as though I'd hocked my life all of these months, had left it with a pawnbroker until the time that I could reclaim it. Now I can walk into the pawnshop with my precious ticket and take it back.

THE WAITING

"Well, you can stop worrying now," I write in a letter to my parents. "I just finished my last mission. Unless the Eighth Air Force changes its policy, I'll be on my way home shortly...Now we'll wait for our orders. When we get these, we'll proceed to another place in England or Scotland. That will be our port of embarkation to the United States. I expect to come home by ship. I think this has been the biggest relief of my whole life, and, believe me, I'm really thankful. Sometimes I really wondered."

The following day we sit on our bunks around the coal stove, trying to keep warm. If we try to venture outside, icy blasts of wind and rain cut into us at the barracks door. We'd braved the chilly weather in the afternoon during a lull in the showers to ride our bicycles over to the base theater where we saw a morbid film starring Ray Milland, *The Uninvited*, a movie that fit perfectly with the gloom of the day.

We expect our orders any day, as they need to get us out to make way for the fresh crews coming in. We might be in the next facility for as much as a month, but we hope for less time.

We also walk over to the hospital to see Podoske and some of the wounded men from other crews, our Purple Heart group. He looks good, but he's tired of lying in bed. We'll be leaving him behind and might never see him again. I'll miss him. We'd been pals since our bomber training in Alexandria, Louisiana. Even though we were different in many ways, we always got along.

"I'll swear I aged a whole year during a single raid sometimes," I write the following day. "It's such a relief now not to worry about having the wits scared out of you or getting that sick feeling in your stomach at what you saw. There was only one thing to do, and that was pray with all your heart."

I think about home constantly, wanting to be there as soon as possible. I even allow myself to think about my plans after the war, even though, in spite of gains by the Allies, the end of the war still seems like a long way off. I'd already made up my mind to go to college, but for the first time I tell my parents in a letter that I would like to try U. C. L. A.

"Tomorrow morning we'll leave this field for the other place," I dash off in a short note to my parents. "That means we're on our way home. How long it will take to get there, I don't know. It may be days, weeks or months, but at least I'm on the way."

* * *

We sit on our bunks in the dull barracks of our "new place," a holding area for crews from groups all over England who have finished their missions. We nibble on the last of the crackers and cheese that my parents had sent. The package had arrived at our base the day before we left, providing the makings for a party the last night at Polebrook. Another cold downpour rattles on the roof and dashes against the windows, the English fall giving us an early taste of winter.

268

The food at the base is terrible. We begin to realize how well we had been fed at Polebrook. They'd given us good food there; perhaps, because they wanted to raise our morale, give us the strength to fly combat missions. We're finished now, so they give us mediocre meals.

We have little to do here but wait. The icy weather restricts us to the barracks where we can only talk to each other. I still feel the joy of just being alive and uninjured, but I and every other man I've talked to burn with a yearning for home, for being reunited with those we love. The incessant waiting around without activities tries us all, puts us on edge.

Five days later, and nothing has changed, including the cold damp weather that keeps us prisoners in the barracks. Many of us feel we're nearly ready for a straightjacket. During breaks in the weather we play a little baseball on the wet grounds. We are shown movies three times a week, but the projector is so faulty, so prone to breakdowns that the films are difficult to enjoy. I find myself often walking down the hall to the drinking fountain where I drink as much water as I can so that later I can make trips to the bathroom, just for something to do.

Our problem is that we know we're going home and know that we'll be given a furlough when we get there, but we can't speed up the process. It's a little like knowing that there are magnificent gifts under the Christmas tree in the next room, but we will not be allowed to enter, and open them until some obscure date weeks from now.

I pen my last letter from England, October 8, 1944. "Well, I'm still here, but I expect to leave within the next few days. In fact, I'm sure of it. When I get to the States, I'll be sent to Monterey, California. I'll get a thirty-day furlough from there...I hope to get home in time for my birthday. Do you know that I haven't seen you in almost ten months, and it will be almost eleven months by the time I get home. That's much too long. And with what I went through, it seems like years."

We walk to church on Sunday morning, a group of us shuffling through a cold fog that has settled around the barracks and blotted out the trees and fields at the edges of our compound. We know we're leaving now, and every man carries that joy and excitement within him. Our warm thoughts about home easily counter the bite of the icy mist.

CROSSING BY SEA

Angry gray clouds race out of the south as our trucks pull into the Liverpool docks, the dull sky darkening the old warehouses and pilings. Our ship, the *U.S.S. Excelsior*, waits at the dock, but the captain is not ready to load us. First they must take on five hundred prisoners of war recently captured in France. I look down as the German soldiers file slowly onto the ship through a large door leading into the hold. Several bare light bulbs hang in the dimness of the entrance. The disheveled men, many of them still wearing their winter coats and dirty-looking caps, must pause at the entrance way for delousing. Several American guards shoot puffs of yellow powder from a "Flit gun", first dusting their hair then shooting it down the backs of their necks and their chests under their clothes. The defeated men appear docile, as though they welcome the treatment, tired of carrying their lice around. I believe that most of them are glad to be out of the war, glad to be going any place where it's peaceful.

I think about how strange it is that I'm about to travel nearly two weeks across the Atlantic with a ship full of the enemy, the people I've been "fighting" from a distance for months. I contemplate the irony of having been in combat and never seeing a German except for the fighter pilot who had bailed out, hanging like a tiny marionette from his parachute, and seeing all of these real Germans now. It had been an impersonal war for me. We'd dropped bombs on factories and probably on people we couldn't see. The flak gunners had never seen our faces either. Now I'm looking at them for the first time, real people with flesh, hair and eyes.

On board now, the ship's crew assigns staterooms to the officers, two to a room in bunk beds. We number no more than thirty. Besides us, the crew and guards, all the rest of the "passengers" are prisoners, who greatly outnumber us. As soon as the last man is aboard, longshoremen free the mooring ropes, and we drift away from the dock. The captain, we are told, is anxious to get into the channel to ride out the storm that is fast approaching.

With the sea already beginning to toss and roil, we walk from our quarters to the dining room where several large tables arranged in a U-shape are draped with crisp white linen tablecloths, gleaming glasses and silverware. Despite the motion of the ship we enjoy a sumptuous meal, far better than the food we had to endure lately.

Anchored just out of Liverpool, the ship rolls in the black night, leaning this way and that in the restless waves. At times I feel I might fall out of my top bunk, but somehow I manage to drift off to sleep, "rocked in the cradle of the deep."

The following morning our ship assembles with at least twenty others and several destroyer escorts for the trip across the Atlantic. The ship's officers give us instructions about the lifesaving equipment aboard and the procedures to be used should German submarines attack us. Even though United States Navy escorts with underwater detecting equipment are with us, there is a chance that a fast-hitting U-boat might be able to launch a torpedo. Although an attack is unlikely, I still have that same feeling that I had in combat, that all is not safe, that danger lurks in some unknown place and will strike when least expected.

We still wallow in the sea, the agitated water sloshing as though stirred in some giant washing machine. Fewer officers show up for meals, all of the absent ones victims of seasickness. Even though my stomach is not perfect, I'm not ill. I look forward to the delicious meals. I refuse to be seasick. I'd foolishly told that psychiatrist back at San Antonio in cadet training that I thought I'd been a little bit seasick once when I'd been on a boat with a dead motor tossing around in the surf. He'd thought that very important, a factor in his trying to ground me. I had never been airsick, even in the roughest weather, and I'll be damned if I'm ever going to be "green around the gills," even on the bounding main!

The seas never settle down. We pound through the waves and rock with the swells. Many of the prisoners who must sleep in hammock-like beds are deathly ill. Those who are able to get up are put to work hammering rust off the inside of the hull. All day long the hollow metallic blows of their hammers beat out a monotonous rhythm. Others work in the kitchen, some of them baking fresh bread each day for our meals.

Gradually the officers begin to return to the table as their systems adjust. During daylight, the Navy destroyers sometimes practice their submarine attack procedures, lobbing depth charges that explode with a thunderous roar and lift huge white fountains of seawater high in the air. Their activity concerns us because we don't know for sure whether they're simply going through their drills or are really after an intruder.

One evening at dinner, a group of German soldiers entertains us with music. The chaplain had arranged the performance, supplying them with accordions, violins, drums and a piano. They play beautifully, as though they'd practiced together for a long time. They present all the old Teutonic favorites, *The Merry Widow Waltz, Tales from the Vienna Woods, Lili Marlene* and others familiar to us then volunteer to render any number that we can suggest. I look at each of the men as they perform, study their faces. They are our adversaries, but most of all they are men, wanting, I believe, what I want, just to be home.

After the concert, the officer in charge of us says, "This was all very nice, and they played well, but let me remind you that these men, only a few days ago, were killing American boys in France. They are still the enemy." Well, I think, that's what soldiers are supposed to do, destroy the enemy. That's what they've always done in all ages whether they wanted to or not.

I stand on the deck, amazed at the size of the swells that we plow through. I had no idea that waves could be so mountainous. At the bottom of the swell I see nothing but water, a watery valley with watery mountains on all sides. We are not a wood chip or even a canoe, but a regular metal seagoing ship, yet we bob about as though we're a mere stick thrown into angry waters by a gleeful little boy having fun. When we rise to the top of the swell, it's like being on the crest of a hill, where we can survey the rest of the ships in our convoy.

I had hardly slept the night before. Our metal helmets had rolled across the floor like hollow bowling balls, pummeling into the walls making an ungodly racket with every tipping of the floor. After much sleepy procrastinating, I had to get up in the night and secure them. As the ship mounted each swell and started down into a valley, the propeller came out of the water, sending a jarring vibration through the whole ship, our beds shaking, the walls shuddering, sleep impossible.

After several more days the seas at last calm down, making life much more pleasant on board. There's not much to do except watch the water go by, but I spend some of my time reading a paperback novel by Sinclair Lewis, *Ann Vickers*. Progress across the Atlantic is very slow, but at least, with every moment, we are getting closer to home.

Some of the prisoners are allowed on the deck with us. They stand around in loose groups, unsmiling and somber, resigned to whatever may happen to them. I don't know what's behind their drawn faces, what thoughts are running through their minds. We walk among them in our clean uniforms and gleaming silver wings, our attire contrasting sharply with their plain rumpled field uniforms. Sometimes they appear to scowl at us, a look of anger or contempt darting from their eyes. I think about how many of them may have had friends or family killed or maimed by American bombs. I feel their hatred there on the deck, like unseen heat rays. I know too that they have done their best to kill Americans in France, but I can't feel any animosity toward them.

A few German soldiers are go-betweens, carrying messages between whoever is in charge of them and the ship's officers. I watch one of them report, a strapping but awkward young man with blondish tousled hair. He noisily stomps into the room, salutes, and snaps together the heels of his boot-like field shoes with a resounding "clack" that I had never heard an American soldier produce.

Finally, after what had seemed like an endless two weeks, we approach New York City. Just outside the harbor we pass a fleet of merchant ships anchored nearby, many of them ready to form convoys carrying war supplies to Europe. "You see that?" asks one of the ship's crew of a curious group of prisoners. "Look at all those ships out there. You know what they're loaded with? War supplies. Tons and tons of them. All on the way to the front. Germany doesn't have a chance!"

The disgruntled captives look at him, mumbling and translating to each other. One of them talks back in German, another crewman translating what he'd said. "Hitler still has more secret revenge weapons. We will win the war with them. You wait and see!"

"He doesn't have shit," scowls the crewman as he stalks off across the deck.

276

Before us is the Statue of Liberty, her hand held high as though she waves a greeting to us. Welcome back! The skyscrapers of Manhattan rise behind the docks in their incredible cluster, like tall crystals pointing heavenward. My God, I've made it back!

THE LAST LEG

After two weeks of adjusting to a pitching, rolling deck, standing on the firm New York City dock seems very secure, but more importantly I'm finally in the United States again. I stroll along the dock with the others, breathing the creosote scent of the pilings, looking down at the green harbor water, occasionally gazing up at the magnificence of the Manhattan skyline. We laugh and talk with each other as we file along the dock, floating on the joy of just being in our own country again.

Officers on the dock guide us to a row of dusty, barn-red interurban cars that were waiting for us. They remind me of our "big red cars" at home. Soon after finding seats in the empty trolleys, we're on our way, rolling along the rails with the hum of electric motors and a faint smell of ozone.

Our trip is short, only across the harbor to Camp Kilmer in New Jersey. The men in charge tell us that we'll be here only a few days, that a troop train will be made up to take us across the country to Monterey.

In our barracks is an officer, a pilot, who doesn't share our joyful effervescence. He mopes around or stands outside the door with his sad countenance. He's not part of our group. The unfortunate fellow is on his way back to England. He'd taken a leave before he'd completed his missions, now he must return to finish them. He says to us, almost in tears, "I can hardly stand the thought of going back to that damned foggy island." I'm glad that I'm not in his shoes.

A few days later we begin our long rail journey home, every click of the wheels over the track joints, meaning that we're that much closer. Our train is a long string of olive-drab Pullman cars with a special army kitchen car in the middle. During mealtime we will file through to fill up our mess trays. I'd never seen the East Coast before and I am surprised that many of the row houses that we pass look just like those we'd left in England. Everything looks English to me, even the low gray clouds that hover over New Jersey. It makes sense, I think, since the British had settled the area so many years before. They had built their houses in the only style they knew.

Almost all transcontinental trains end up in Chicago, the greatest railroad center in the country. From there the rails fan out in all directions. After the Pennsylvania Railroad hands off our train to the Chicago, Burlington and Quincy, it storms across fertile Illinois farmland, trailing plumes of black smoke as we head west.

The CB&Q transfers our train to the Denver and Rio Grande Western after it reaches Denver, where the plains reach the eastern flank of the Rockies. The D&RGW, after hauling us over the mountains, gives us to the Western Pacific at Salt Lake City for the trip over the Sierras to Oakland. Once we reach the Sierras I begin to feel the excitement of being in California again, of being home, the electricity of it running through my body. Our train sweeps through the Feather River Canyon, following the waterway that had carved it. We relax in the Pullmans as we gaze up at the granite crags and cliffs.

At a point almost to the western Sierra foothills the train suddenly stops. There are no stations in sight, only the lonely rails winding around the flank of the mountains. None of us, anxious to get home, understands the delay. After a half hour, with still no movement, some of the restless get off and walk towards toward the locomotive. Curious about what's happened, I hustle down the steps, walk along the train on the dirt and rock ballast. I pass the hissing steam locomotive, walking by the largest driving wheels and rods I'd ever seen. Steam curls around its cylinders as I look ahead to see a work crew putting the finishing touches on a new rail. A loose boulder had rolled down the mountain before our train arrived, bending the old one. With the track gang finished several others and I hustle along the track to our car, the train pulling out almost as soon as we sit down.

In the Bay Area the Southern Pacific couples on to our train for the final short distance to Monterey. We steam out over the rickety branch line, the roadbed and rails badly out of shape. The Pullman cars rock and sway so much that it almost feels as though we're back on the ship. We pass Fort Ord and the vast sand dunes, finally easing into the old Monterey station. Trucks transport us to the venerable Presidio among the dark cypress trees on the hill. We're to spend the night there, then be released at the end of the next day for our thirty-day furloughs.

"Hello Mom. This is Norman," I say as I lean in close to the telephone mouthpiece.

"Oh," she answers with trembling in her voice. "Is it really you? Where are you?"

I can hardly believe that I'm hearing the sound of my mother's voice, that sweet sound that I often wondered whether I would ever hear again. "Well, I'm in Monterey now. Just got here. We have to stay tonight, but tomorrow they're going to let us go on our leaves. I already have my train ticket for the *Lark*. I'll catch it in Salinas tomorrow, and be in Los Angeles the next morning about eight o'clock."

"I'm so glad you're home," she says. "We were so worried about you."

I sit up all night on the *Lark*, the overnight train from San Francisco to Los Angeles, but I'm too excited to sleep. I think about nothing but home, seeing everyone, telling them all about my adventures, stories that I could not write to them in my letters. Now and then I doze off, hypnotized by the regular rhythm of the wheels clicking over the rails, but I soon wake up again. My head feels swollen with all that I have to tell them, every experience that I had had pumping up my mind until I think it will explode.

I wonder about how I will be with them after so long a time, my life having recently been so different from theirs. I wonder if all that fear and worry, all those hellish times that I had lived through, had taken their toll on me. Would they find me different from the son they sent off so many months ago? If they should see a different person from their mind's vision of me, how would they handle it? I know I've lost a little hair, have aged at least two years in one. How will they be with me?

But I'm the same son inwardly, and they, with their unreserved love will see that. They'll be as glad to see me, as I am to see them. They'll all be there, waiting.

The train rolls into Union Station on time, the same place I'd left months before and the one that my dad had taken me to when it opened only five years before. I grab my bag and head down the station platform, brimming over with excitement, a mixture of eager anticipation and a touch of fear. Down in the passenger tunnel I walk with all the others who have just gotten off the train, the murmur of their voices and the shuffling of their clothing, the clicking of their shoes echoing in the long passageway. With the tunnel ending, I see the silhouettes of my mother, my father, my sister Charline and my friend Barbara. Their shadowed forms become familiar bodies and faces as I walk closer, and I slowly melt into their warmth and love once again.

LIST OF MISSIONS FLOWN

Charles N. Stevens (0704242)

1	June 14, 1944 Le Bourget, France
2	15 Angouleme, France
3	18 Hamburg, Germany
4	20 Watten, France
5	22 Rouen, France
6	23 Abbeville, France (near, Noball)
7	24 Crepy, France (Noball)
8	25 Toulouse, France
9	28 Loon Couvron, France
10	July 4 Saumur, France
11	6 Bertreville St. Ouen, France (Noball)
12	11 Munich, Germany
13	12 Munich, Germany
14	13 Munich, Germany
15	16 Stuttgart, Germany
16	18 Peenemunde, Germany
17	19 Augsburg, Germany

18	21 Schweinfurt, Germany
19	24 Normandy Area, France (Tactical)
20	31 Munich, Germany
21	Aug 8 St. Sylvian (Area) (Tactical)
22	11 Brest, France (Tactical)
23	13 Ouviers, France (Tactical)
24	16 Schkeuditz, Germany
25	18 Namur, Belgium
26	24 Weimar, Germany
27	25 Aenin-Lietard, France
28	27 Berlin, Germany (Aborted)
29	30 Kiel, Germany
30	Sep 8 Ludwigshafen, Germany
31	12 Ruhland, Germany
32	17 Groesbeck, Holland (near) (Tactical)
33	19 Soest, Germany
34	22 Kassel, Germany

ABOUT THE AUTHOR

Charles N. Stevens, or Norm as his friends call him, grew up in Inglewood, California. At 18 he joined the Army Air Corps. He entered in April 1943 and was discharged after the war in October 1946. He served as a bombardier on a B-17 in the 8th Air Force, 351st Bomb Group, at Polebrook, England during the summer and early fall of 1944. He finished his tour of duty, completing 34 bombing missions over Germany and occupied France, Belgium and Holland.

After returning from overseas he trained as a radar bombardier at Langley Field, Virginia and Williams Field, Arizona. He was to be assigned to a B-29 crew for duty in the Pacific when the war ended.

Following the war he enrolled at U.C.L.A., graduating with a BA in psychology. After a series of graduate courses, he earned his teaching credential. Over a span of 32 years he taught general science and mathematics in junior high school and English and literature in high school. While teaching he earned a master's degree in English at California State College at Los Angeles.

He has two sons by a previous marriage, Jeffry L. Stevens and Greg E. Stevens and five grandchildren—Brenda, Sharon, Eric, Michael and Beth.

He retired in 1984 and has lived a life of reading, writing, traveling and being a grandfather. He lives with his wife, Dolores Seidman, in Monterey Park, California where they have resided for 32 years.

CPSIA information can be obtained
at www.ICGtesting.com
Printed in the USA
FSOW02n1538120416
19122FS

9 781414 045634